ICT and adult literacy, numeracy and ESOL

Harvey Mellar, Maria Kambouri,
Mariana Sanderson and Victoria Pavlou

CONTENTS

This report is funded by the Department for Education and Skills as part of the national strategy for improving adult literacy and numeracy skills. The views expressed are those of the authors and do not necessarily reflect those of the Department.

Preface

ICT is becoming essential to work and daily life; it is changing the nature of work and the skills required in the workplace. The government 21st Century Skills Strategy states that "Basic ICT will become a third area of adult basic skills, alongside literacy and numeracy within our **Skills for Life** programme."[1] NRDC is working with organisations involved in developing ICT skills and the use of ICT to develop literacy, numeracy and ESOL. Indeed all these skills are becoming inextricably linked:

> "It is only in the integration of technological skills and cognitive skills, such as traditional literacy, numeracy, and problem solving, that one can adequately define ICT literacy" International ICT Literacy Panel (2002)[2]

Research has shown that ICT is increasingly required in the workplace particularly with numeracy but also with reading and writing. NRDC research is looking at ICT as a dimension of NRDC's research and development programmes across Skills for life. ICT is also impacting on the nature of literacy and numeracy practices in daily life at home and in the community, And new digital literacies involving multi-modal forms of expression are emerging. Of course ICT is not just about computers and current interest in m-learning and digital video technology is growing.

At NRDC we are also taking the work forward in a study of effective practice in teaching and learning ICT which has been developed as part of a linked suite of studies looking at which approaches to teaching and learning help learners to achieve. The studies focus on reading, writing, ESOL, numeracy and ICT: with ICT also a feature of each of the other four studies. The ICT study looks at achievement both in ICT skills and in literacy, numeracy and ESOL and incorporates a range of technologies including m-learning.

Note on terminology

We use the term Information and Communications Technology (ICT) here to refer to the use of computers and other digital technologies within education and our focus is on the way in which these technologies are used to support learning and teaching rather than on the technologies themselves. The preferred term within the Further Education sector has been Information and Learning Technologies (ILT), and the preferred term in recent DfES documents is e-learning. The tutors and learners that we talked to tended to be uncomfortable with the term e-learning and associated this term with distance education in Higher Education. We found the term ICT well understood and glossed this as ILT for some audiences.

---

1. 21st Century Skills Realising our potential (2003) London:DfES
2. International ICT Literacy Panel (2002), Digital Transformation: A Framework for ICT Literacy Educational Testing Service (ETS), Princeton, NJ, Available from: http://www.ets.org/resesarch/ictliteracy.

Summary

Previous studies carried out by the Institute of Education (for example Mellar et al., 2001) have provided a broad picture of practice in the use of information and communications technology (ICT) in adult literacy, numeracy and English for Speakers of Other Languages (ESOL). This research found some positive signs, but suggested there was a long way to go if the expectations of the impact of ICT on learning for this group of learners were to be met. Further research was needed to discover more effective ways of using ICT to improve learning for learners with basic skills needs in order to support a move beyond present practice. The aim of this present study was to carry out detailed observational research in classrooms: to collect, review and analyse existing practice; examine how the use of ICT had impacted on the teaching and learning of basic skills in these classrooms; and so to begin to more closely identify the factors involved in effective teaching with ICT in the areas of adult literacy, numeracy and ESOL. The findings of this project will inform an intervention study, which will generate hypotheses about effective use of ICT in adult literacy, numeracy and ESOL and then develop and test these strategies.

The main findings of the present study were:

Using ICT

The predominant pattern of activity was for learners to use a desktop computer on their own, with the tutor either presenting to the whole class or involved in discussion with groups or individuals. About half of the observed activity involved the use of office software and half the use of educational software. The majority of ICT use was directed towards practice, but some use related to the creation of new materials or accessing information (this latter activity tended to be associated with students working in small groups).

Integrating ICT

Various activities involved the use of ICT to support the teaching of basic skills. At one extreme, ICT was seen as just another teaching tool and the technological demands were kept to a minimum. At the other extreme, ICT skills were seen as important elements of new literacies.

Teaching styles

The majority of teaching consisted of group presentation followed by an activity supported by individual tutoring, though some sessions consisted exclusively of individual tutoring. The tutors spent about half their time talking to the class as a whole and about half talking with small groups and individuals. The amount of time devoted by tutors to quiet observation of learners was quite small. However, on some occasions tutors sat back and avoided intervening as part of a conscious process of encouraging student independence and autonomy.

Teaching with ICT

Teachers adapted the use of ICT to their own style of teaching. Different patterns of ICT use were found in numeracy, literacy and ESOL. Tutors' level of ICT skills had an impact on their ability to make effective use of the technology. It was also true that specific characteristics of certain technologies affected the way in which these were used in the classroom.

Teaching ICT skills

Talking about a procedure, demonstrating it and then asking the students to try it on their own was the most frequent method adopted to teach ICT skills. A minority of tutors encouraged learners to experiment and discover for themselves how the software worked.

Learning styles

The visual elements of ICT presentation were useful to many learners, but we saw few attempts to accommodate students' learning styles in other ways. Individual and whole group work were the dominant styles but small group work was encouraged in some literacy and ESOL classes.

Recommendations for practice

Observed good practice

We saw a range of what appeared to us to be good practice in the use of ICT in adult literacy and numeracy. We list here the main points that came from our observations.

- Clear lesson aims, explained and/or negotiated with learners at the start of the session, coupled with a review of what has been learnt at the end of the session. (Whilst perhaps always good practice, this has particular importance in directing the learners' attention to what they are expected to learn from the use of the technology and how they are expected to do this.)
- A combination of multiple ways of providing information, such as demonstration through a data projector, handouts and materials stored on the computer network.
- Providing opportunities for peer learning both through small group work and through the projection of learners' work for whole class discussion.
- Flexibility in classroom management terms – accepting collaboration when it occurs naturally, directing learners to specific reinforcement activities if necessary and sometimes avoiding intervention as part of a process of encouraging student independence and autonomy.
- For classes adopting the 'instructional tool' approach – a close integration of literacy and numeracy learning objectives with ICT learning objectives and the use of technology in a wide variety of ways throughout the session.
- For classes adopting the 'complement to instruction approach' – careful preparation of materials and thorough familiarisation with teaching materials (both those that will be used, and those that might be used) before using them with learners. Consolidation of learning through doing the same tasks with and without ICT.

Areas for development

Approaches to using technology

- Tutors need to consider why they are using ICT and match the way that they use the technology to their aims. Ginsburg's (1998) discussion of the range of approaches to using technology in basic skills education may be useful here.
- Teaching also needs to address the changing nature of literacies in the digital age, new forms of relationship between media are being created and new genres of writing are developing.

Teaching

- A wider range of technologies and ways of using them needs to be explored. For example, we saw no use of interactive whiteboards. All use that we saw of data-projectors were tutor controlled – we saw no examples of learners taking control of projectors. Digital cameras, digital video, personal digital assistants (PDAs) and mobile phones are just some of the other technologies that could be explored. A wider range of software should also be explored – there is much useful practice in schools that could suggest possibilities.

■ Greater experimentation with teaching styles and forms of classroom management should be encouraged. Does a highly structured approach encourage dependence? Does too loosely structured an approach run the risk of learner frustration?

■ How do we stop ICT getting in the way of learning? How do we identify learners' ICT skills and finding effective methods of teaching ICT skills (whether class teaching, peer learning or the use of effective support materials) that would teach the skills without the inefficiency of individual tutoring.

■ Greater attention needs to be given to the range of learning styles and learner preferences and ways in which ICT might be used to address these.

Collaboration

■ Work is needed to develop appropriate ways for learners to work effectively together using ICT. This needs to go beyond allowing learners to work together towards defining structures and roles for collaborative work. How do we prevent the requirements of assessment getting in the way of the development of collaborative work?

Teaching ICT

■ The issue of how to teach ICT needs to be addressed more explicitly. Tutors who adopt a wider range of strategies for developing learners' literacy and numeracy skills sometimes adopt a purely didactic form of teaching when approaching ICT skills. There is a need for a structured curriculum for ICT skills and for ways of determining progression. Learners need to be supported in their exploration of ICT.

Recommendations for policy

Whilst this study is limited in scope – being a detailed study of a small group of tutors – it is possible to interpret these results within the context of the other studies that we have carried out in order to derive some recommendations for policy. Our study concentrated on a small group of tutors who were working within a Pathfinder Consortium, who were keen on using ICT, were identified by the Consortium as making good use of ICT and had their colleges' support in using ICT in the classroom.

We found that most of these tutors were relatively new to the use of ICT and their practice demonstrated that they were still at the early stages of developing approaches to using ICT in their teaching. They needed support in order to develop these skills further. It is a reasonable hypothesis that if this is the case for this group of tutors then it is going to be even more of an issue for tutors more generally. Our work with a range of tutors in **learndirect** centres (Kambouri, Mellar et al., 2003) has shown that there are difficulties in training ICT specialists to take on basic skills teaching and so it is probably more effective to give basic skills tutors training in ICT use and time to prepare their sessions using ICT rather than attempting to train ICT specialists to support basic skills. We therefore recommend:

Development of effective tutor training in the use of ICT in basic skills provision and support (including funding) for tutors during this training.

Again, the tutors we observed were in relatively privileged positions compared to many of their colleagues using ICT in basic skills teaching and had strong institutional support, nevertheless we observed a number of restrictions on their use of ICT due to difficulties with the ICT infrastructure – particularly the computer network – and were aware at times that the teaching of basic skills was sometimes at the end of the queue for provision. Earlier work (Mellar, Kambouri et al., 2001) has shown this to be a widespread issue. We therefore recommend:

Further development of ICT infrastructure (particularly computer networks) and higher priority to be given to provision of ICT for basic skills teaching.

The tutors we were working with were enthusiastic about using ICT in their teaching and more knowledgeable about ICT than many of the tutors we have talked to in other studies. Nevertheless their teaching as we observed it showed that they were often unclear about what aspects of ICT were valuable to their learners, there was little attention given to progression in ICT skills and little assessment that learners had achieved ICT objectives (as distinct from the literacy, numeracy and ESOL objectives). This study was carried out before the development of the standards for ICT as a skill for life, and these standards do now provide a basis to enable tutors to ensure progression in the development of ICT skills (something that was lacking at the time of this study).The range of ways in which ICT was introduced into the classroom that we observed both in this study and in our other studies shows that there is little agreement amongst tutors about what should be taught in this area. We therefore recommend:

Further development of the ICT skills curriculum and assessment methods. Further consideration and debate about the nature of an ICT skills curriculum.

Main elements of research

In collaboration with a group of eight tutor-researchers within the East London Pathfinder Consortium, we generated a range of themes that we wished to investigate and examined a variety of possible observational methods (including video capture and software for capturing learner interaction with the computer). By working closely with the tutor-researchers in this way invaluable insights were gained into present practice. The main observational methods that were finally developed and used were structured observation instruments for observing tutors and, to a lesser extent, learners, in the classroom. We carried out detailed observations in 11 classrooms using ICT in adult literacy, numeracy or ESOL. On average each class was observed four times times over a two-month period, three observations concentrating on the tutor and a further observation session devoted to learners.

The tutors we observed were all drawn from Further Education Colleges within the East London Pathfinder Consortium. We chose tutors who were making particular use of ICT in their teaching and who were seen by their colleges as 'early-adopters', people who were keen to explore the potentials of ICT in learning and teaching. Working closely with these tutor-researchers, we drew up procedures for carrying out classroom observations and then made detailed observations of classrooms using ICT in adult literacy, numeracy or ESOL.

Observations were carried out by research officers and by the eight tutor-researchers who observed each other's sessions. The first level accounts generated were fed back to the group of tutor-researchers for further discussion. The structured observation instruments have generated both quantitative surface level descriptions and qualitative data, which we then used to develop detailed accounts of each tutor's classroom. We then interviewed each tutor about the detailed account we had produced of his or her lessons.

Background and rationale of research

There are strong expectations that ICT can contribute to the development of *Skills for Life* provision. Previous work looking at ICT and adult literacy and numeracy (e.g. Hopey, 1998, Mellar et al., 2001) has mainly been based on surveys or interviews with managers, tutors and learners and whilst this has given us an insight into some of the principal variables that may be involved, we have little detailed account of what tutors actually do when they are using ICT for adult literacy and numeracy. In this study, we set out to develop a methodology to carry out an observational study in order to begin to identify more closely the factors involved in effective teaching with ICT in the areas of adult literacy, numeracy and ESOL. This study concentrated on the use of ICT within college settings as we were simultaneously carrying out work within other projects looking at ICT and *Skills for Life* within **learndirect** centres, prisons and community provision.

Acknowledgements

This research would not have been possible without the co-operation of many people and we would like to thank everyone who has participated in and supported this project.

We would like to thank in particular the tutors with whom we worked: Judith Beer, Sean Gubbins, Jenik Nazarian, Camilla Nightingale, Jane Peckham, Eugene Smith, Graciano Soares and Peter Townsend and special thanks to Jenny Barrett – the East London Pathfinder Coordinator. Our thanks go also to the managers and staff of the colleges that we worked in and to all the learners who allowed us to observe their classes in action.

We would also like to thank Susan Morse at the Institute of Education for the excellent administrative support and Eric Hadley for prompt technical advice and support throughout the project.

For their valuable comments on the final draft we would like to thank John Bynner, Jill Attewell and Jenny Hunt as well as Andrew Lincoln and his colleagues from DfES and also all those patient participants in conferences and workshops around the country who have always inspired and constructively critiqued this work.

Finally our thanks go to everyone who as involved in producing this report, in particular Sophy Toohey.

Independent peer review
This report was read and independently peer reviewed by Jill Attewell (LSDA), John Bynner (Institute of Education, University of London) and Jenny Hunt (Schemata).

Introduction
Background and aims of the study

The **Skills for Life** strategy identifies the importance of ICT for improving adult literacy and numeracy and there are considerable expectations that ICT will play an important role in delivering these skills. ICT is seen as a motivator, as opening up wider access to learning, as providing new ways of teaching and learning and now as a basic skill.

In recent years, the Institute of Education has carried out a number of evaluation studies of the use of ICT (including interactive digital TV, CD-ROMs, web-based and hybrid technologies) in the teaching of adult literacy and numeracy for the Basic Skills Agency as part of European Union (EU) funded projects. We have also carried out a study for Ufi/**learndirect** on the effectiveness of learning through ICT for learners with basic skills needs that combined qualitative methods with a quantitative study on learning gains and as part of this project, produced a guide for practitioners (Ufi 2001).

This earlier research found some positive signs, but suggested there was a long way to go if the expectations of the impact of ICT on learning for this group are to be met. Further research is needed in order to support a move beyond present practice and to discover more effective ways of using ICT to improve learning for learners with basic skills needs. The existing research both our own and that of others (e.g. e.g. Hopey 1998, Mellar et al., 2001) had mainly been based on surveys or interviews, and to some degree on pre-and post-testing of literacy and numeracy skills and whilst it gave an insight into some of the principal variables that may be involved it gave little detailed account of what tutors actually do when they are using ICT for adult literacy and numeracy.

The aim of this present study was to carry out detailed observational research in classrooms: to collect, review and analyse existing practice; examine how the use of ICT had impacted on the teaching and learning of basic skills in these classrooms; and so to begin to more closely identify the factors involved in effective teaching with ICT in the areas of adult literacy and numeracy. The findings of this project will inform an intervention study, which will generate a series of hypotheses about effective use and develop and then test effective strategies for the use of ICT in the areas of adult literacy, numeracy and ESOL.

The tutors we observed were all drawn from Further Education Colleges within the East London Pathfinder Consortium[3]. We chose tutors who were making particular use of ICT in their teaching and who were seen by their colleges as 'early-adopters', people who were keen to explore the potentials of ICT in learning and teaching. Working closely with these tutor-researchers, we drew up procedures for carrying out classroom observations and then made detailed observations of classrooms using ICT in adult literacy, numeracy or ESOL.

The context of this particular study is deliberately narrow, concentrating on provision within further education colleges because we have carried out a series of other studies in other

---

3. A consortium of five FE Colleges led the East London Pathfinder project with involvement from local community and voluntary organisations. The lead organisations were: Tower Hamlets College, Lewisham College, City and Islington College, Newham College of Further Education, Hackney Community College, East London Advanced Technology Training, Hackney Partners In Learning.

contexts in parallel with the work reported here. These studies have looked at such questions as the effectiveness of the **learndirect *Skills for Life*** materials and support system (Kambouri, Mellar et al., 2003), the role of computer games (Kambouri, Schott et al., 2003), the use of web-authoring and animation tools in health education for young offenders and the role of ICT in voluntary organisations and community based provision. We have also produced a guide for the use of laptops in basic skills provision (NRDC 2003).

The project ran from July 2002 to March 2003, with the main data collection phase taking place between October 2002 and January 2003.

The research team for this project was made up as follows:

Project Directors: Dr Harvey Mellar and Dr Maria Kambouri.

Research Officers: Dr Mariana Sanderson and Dr Victoria Pavlou.

East London Pathfinder Co-ordinator: Jenny Barrett.

Tutor-Researchers: Judith Beer, Sean Gubbins, Jenik Nazarian, Jane Peckham, Camilla Nightingale, Eugene Smith, Graciano Soares and Peter Townsend.

Methodology

Preparation

Review of research

In early 2002, the Learning and Skills Development Agency had begun to carry out a review of research on 'The impact of ICT upon literacy and numeracy skills of young people and adults with basic skills needs' for the DfES. Unfortunately this review did not become available during the time of this study, but we were involved in the Advisory Group for the study and are therefore aware of the literature that was being identified.

East London Pathfinder Consortium

Before the project began the directors spent some time visiting practitioners to identify possible partners and identify the questions that the practitioners saw as important. One particularly productive meeting in generating questions was a break out session at a meeting of the East London Pathfinder Consortium and the questions generated there are outlined below. The present study does not pick up on all of these questions, but these formed the basis from which we developed, with the tutor-researchers, the research questions that we were to examine.

Pedagogies
- Do learners learn using ICT?
- Exactly how do learners learn using ICT?
- How does learning take place?
- ICT is motivational – but does it translate into learning?
- How can individual learning styles be supported? (There are a variety of perspectives on learning styles, some stressing aspects such as sensory modes, with others stressing dimensions such as dependence/independence.)
- Is there a threshold literacy level for a learner to be helped by ICT?
- What is the impact of ICT on learners with disabilities, are there thresholds here?
- How does the age of the learner impact on their learning using ICT?
- Could ICT have an impact on thinking processes/ways of thinking?
- Does ICT encourage students to take risks and experiment more?
- What are the best ways of combining students' learning through different means?
- How important is collaborative learning?
- Classroom management – what are the optimum student numbers for classes working with ICT?
- How does ICT impact on students' learning outside the classroom? Are learners empowered?

Digital literacies
- It is no longer a question of simply using ICT to support literacy and numeracy goals, the nature of literacies is itself changed by ICT and learners are living in this world of new literacies. What is the appropriate teaching response to this change?

Assessment
- Does ICT help as an assessment tool?
- How effective are ICT placement tests?

Materials/technologies

- How effective are different types of materials?
- Is the use of ICT for learner self-expression more effective than a more didactic use?

Staffing and training issues

- Staffing – double skilled versus double staffing – ICT/basic skills – ICT tutors learn basic skills versus upskilling basic skills tutors.
- Funding as motivation to improve skills of part-time teachers to meet new standards.
- What technology do tutors/learners need?

Identification of centres and tutor-researchers

We wished to look at the use of ICT in a range of contexts, in particular:

- Courses supported by use of 'office software' – e.g. word-processing, spreadsheets and the Internet[4].
- Courses supported by educational software designed specifically for the teaching of basic skills.
- Literacy.
- English for speakers of other languages.
- Numeracy.

The study was carried out in centres forming part of the East London Pathfinder Consortium. Working with the Pathfinder ICT Co-ordinator we identified a group of eight tutors who would cover the range of uses of ICT that we wanted to see and who would be willing to work with the project. The eight tutors were chosen because they were already integrating ICT into basic skills teaching and were considered to be doing so successfully; many were ILT (Information and Learning Technologies) champions within their colleges. They came from five different providers, all colleges within London. These eight tutor-researchers together with the Pathfinder Co-ordinator formed an integral part of the research team, something that we felt greatly added to the quality and validity of the data and to the usefulness of the conclusions drawn. The tutor-researchers were to be involved at every level of the project: setting the project goals, contributing to the development of the observation criteria, testing out the criteria, carrying out observations of other tutors' classrooms, giving feedback on the results and the project report.

The project was organised around three one-day workshops in which the whole team participated. The tutor-researchers were provided with five days of teaching cover to allow them to attend these meetings and to carry out observations.

As a pilot, we videotaped three classroom sessions and in subsequent workshops with the tutor-researchers we discussed and analysed those tapes. Tutors were not always comfortable with the idea of videotaping their sessions and so this was not used as a method of data capture in the project. It was widely agreed that these initial tapes had been a very useful resource to act as focus for discussion throughout the project.

---

4. This would usually be Microsoft Office software, but in the term 'office software' we also include the use of some non-Microsoft products that have the same functions. Particular examples would be the use of non-Microsoft web-authoring tools and web-browsers.

First workshop

The workshop started with a discussion of the aims of the project and a presentation by the Project Directors on the results of their previous projects. The workshop went on to share tutors' current practice and to outline the issues and problems that needed to be addressed. The videos that had been made of teaching sessions formed a very useful resource for discussion – both of present practice and research issues.

The workshop also began a discussion of methods of capturing data. The trial use of videotaping had shown that, at least initially, some classes and tutors found it hard to relax (though others found no problem). Other tutors pointed out the impracticality of videotaping sessions in small rooms and highlighted the objections of Muslims (who formed a significant proportion of learners in the classes observed) to being photographed. Therefore, it was decided not to pursue this direction in general, though some classrooms might be videotaped. The workshop was itself videotaped and this video was found to be a useful training resource for one of the research officers who was appointed after this workshop had taken place.

Research questions

The first workshop enabled us to define the themes that the research team saw as relevant in addressing the general aim 'to carry out detailed observational research in classrooms: to collect, review and analyse existing practice; examine how the use of ICT had impacted on the teaching and learning of basic skills in these classrooms; and so to begin to more closely identify the factors involved in effective teaching with ICT in the areas of adult literacy and numeracy'. These themes were:

- Curriculum
  - Relationship of ICT and content objectives.
  - Learning objectives of tutors/learning goals of learners.
  - Accreditation of ICT as well as literacy and numeracy.
  - Difference between ESOL and literacy.

- ICT
  - ICT as a possible barrier.
  - ICT as a basic skill – digital literacies.
  - ICT as a subject in itself – the vocabulary of ICT.
  - Technological breakdown.

- Learners
  - Learning preferences.
  - Individual and collaborative working.
  - Feedback.
  - Literacy level of the learners.
  - Specific characteristics of THIS audience (adults/basic skills).

- Teachers
  - Relationship between ICT and teaching styles.
  - Classroom management.
  - Meta-language of the classroom.
  - Management of open learning.

Development of observation methods

Second tutor workshop

The second workshop was principally concerned with the issues of data capture, methods of observation, number and timing of visits and tutor-researcher involvement.

While videotaping was presented as a possible way of collecting data during the first workshop, after discussion with the tutors this method was abandoned. In order to capture more detail of learners' use of ICT we investigated the use of software that would capture interaction with the computer such as Spector[5] and Camtasia[6]. However, this was also abandoned as it was likely to present problems for use on many of the already overloaded computer networks in the colleges and it was not a high priority in this stage of the research, which was principally concerned with classroom behaviour rather than individual learner behaviour.

Discussion concentrated on how research questions identified in the previous workshop were to be incorporated into the observational schedules and the number and kind of observations to be carried out. It was decided that each tutor would prepare a pre-session report outlining the learning objectives and the place of ICT within their lessons. Then, lessons would be viewed on three or four occasions, with at least one observation being undertaken by one of the tutor-researchers. Whilst most of the researcher observations would be of the class as a whole, one of the observations for each class would look at the learners.

Observation schedules and observations

The tutors were asked to complete a pre-session report setting out their goals for the session (see **Tutor's pre-session report** in Appendix 3).

The main classroom observation instrument developed incorporated elements of both highly structured observations and more narrative descriptions. This instrument went through a number of developmental stages starting with a rather general one and developing into a more specific one – for the final version see **Classroom observation schedule** in Appendix 3. The schedule has two aspects: a structured coding to be carried out at five-minute intervals and a section for a more general narrative account together with a column for comments linking the observations to the learning objectives identified in the pre-session report. These instruments were initially piloted on the videotapes of session that we had recorded and then in a number of partial class observations.

A definition of the coding for this structured element of the observation is presented in the form of a systemic network (for an account of systemic networks see Bliss et al., 1983). The systemic network notation used employs three symbols:

Symbol		Instruction
	A B C	Code each of the variables A, B, C.
	D E	Select one of D and E.
	F G	Repeat selection as often as necessary.

Figure 1: Systematic network for the classroom observation

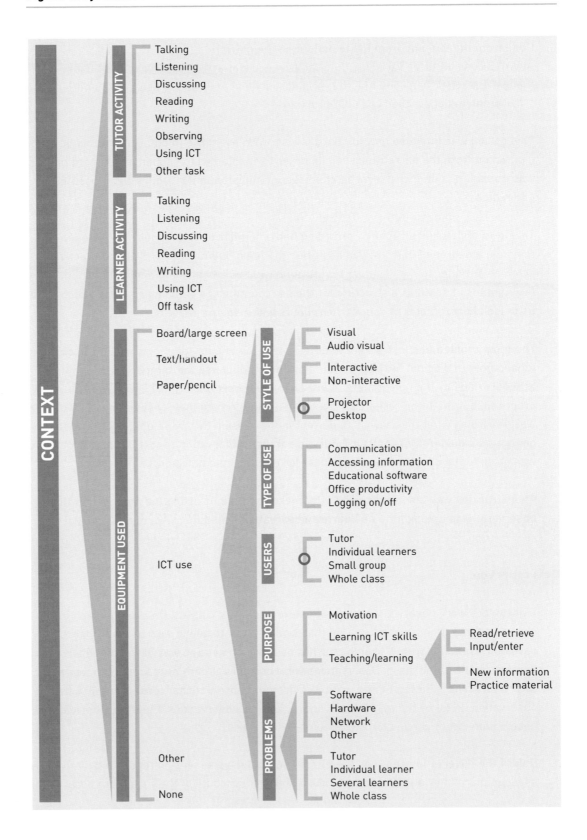

5. http://www.spectorsoft.com/ – accessed 18 May 2004
6. http://www.techsmith.com/products/studio/default.asp – accessed 18 May 2004

The coding rules were:

a) Code predominant activity over last five minutes.
b) Code from the left, and from top to bottom, in the network.
c) ALWAYS code all three variables: tutor activity, learner activity and equipment used.
d) If any ICT is used then code ALL the variables: style of use, type of use, users and purpose.
e) If ICT problems occur then code ICT problems.

This coding was intended only to take a few seconds every five minutes and not to be a major distraction from the narrative coding. In order to enable this to happen an element of practice was necessary, but once the researchers were familiar with the coding this presented few difficulties.

This level of detailed structured recording had a number of advantages. It enabled us to maintain a degree of objectivity in capturing the main outlines of the classroom activities, it acted as a trigger to the observer to reflect on what was happening in the classroom every five minutes, it acted as a structure for their accounts and it acted as an index which enabled us to look for examples of specific behaviours within the narrative accounts.

The most problematic instrument to develop was the one for tutor-researchers to observe other tutors. It was not felt appropriate that they should use the complex observational schedule used by the researchers. A pro-forma for observing critical events was initially proposed, but the tutor-researchers opted instead to record their observations in a more open way, recording what they saw as important in the session they were observing. The team generated a guidance sheet (see **Tutor-researcher observation report** in Appendix 3), which was given to the observers as a\top sheet for them to take notes on.

An instrument was also developed for learner observations listing the main points that observers were to look for (see **Learner observation schedule** in Appendix 3).

Data collection

Eight tutors were observed working with eleven different classes. On average each tutor was observed three times over a two-month period in order to gain a view of the learners' developing practice with ICT[7] and a further observation session was devoted to observing the learners in the same class. Observations were carried out both by research officers and by tutor-researchers. In total there were 24 classroom observations (constituting 774 five-minute observation units) by the researchers and 12 learner observations. Eleven further classroom observations were carried out by the tutor-researchers.[8]

Before the observation sessions the tutors completed a pre-session report and often provided a lesson plan. After an observation a short summary account of the classroom observation

---

7. That is any changes of use in technology in the classroom over time, either as part of a planned progression or arising from greater practice and familiarity. We were particularly concerned to capture the tutor's perspective on how this practice should be developing rather than tracking the achievements of individual learners.
8. The observations of the tutor-researchers of each other's practice were extremely valuable in generating additional insights beyond those generated by the observations of the researchers. However these observations were reported in a range of ways by the tutors, and as colleagues they may not have been as impartial as outside observers in their reports. In interpreting the observational data, therefore, the main emphasis of the research was on the observations done by the researchers, and the observational data from the tutor-researchers was used to question, clarify and extend these interpretations.

was created and sent to the tutor for comments. It had been hoped that this would generate a negotiated account of the session, but in practice there were relatively few comments – though there was some useful feedback. It was felt that it would be best to interview tutors immediately or shortly after the session observed, but, in practice, this turned out to be impossible because of the time constraints on the tutors.

Tutor-researchers varied greatly in the way in which they approached the classroom observations, most tutors took on the observing role, but some chose to work with groups of learners. The style of reporting also varied – some were timed narratives others carefully organised around specific themes. All, however, found the experience useful from the perspective of their own professional development and almost all reported that it was the first time that they had seen other tutors teaching with ICT.

Third workshop

A third workshop was carried out towards the end of the observations in January 2003 and this gave the research team an opportunity to reflect on the data collection process (and in particular on the observational instruments) and on the data collected. The team collectively developed thumbnail accounts of each of the classrooms observed, calling on evidence from the researchers, the tutors as observers and the tutors as teachers. This served to deepen the understanding of what was happening in the classrooms and orient the researchers to the data before starting on the data analysis.

Analysis and report writing

The qualitative data for each tutor's class was first summarised under a set of headings derived from the research questions using a pro-forma (see **Pro-forma for summaries of observational data** in Appendix 3). These summaries of observational data were then developed into a series of 11 case studies (six of these are given in full in Appendix 1). These were analysed with the qualitative data analysis program Nvivo and comparisons made between tutors. The quantitative data was entered into the statistical analysis package SPSS and analysed in terms of frequencies of categories both for the group as a whole and separately by tutor. Cross tabulations were carried out in order to identify whether there were relationships between the variables and where these were found they are reported below. The insights from the qualitative and quantitative analyses were then brought together and the results presented to the tutor-researchers for comment. These comments were then incorporated into the final report.

The classes observed

The 11 classes observed are listed below, together with the label used for these classes within these accounts and the second column gives the somewhat shorter label that is used in the figures.

Classess observed and label	Short label
PT – ESOL & ICT – Level 1 This was an ESOL (Level 1) and ICT class. All sessions included both ICT and language objectives and the teaching of ICT was closely integrated with the language learning objectives. There were 20 learners enrolled on this course, and the usual attendance was about 15. The class lasted two hours.	ESOL (& ICT) – PT
GS1 – ESOL & ICT – entry 3 This was a non-assessed IT option within an ESOL Entry level 3 course. The overall aim of the course was for learners to develop a way of presenting their language work, developing documents in Word, then importing them into Front Page and then publishing them as personal websites in WebCT. There were 15 learners enrolled on this course and the usual attendance was about ten. The class lasted one and a half hours.	ESOL (& ICT) – GS1
GS2 – ESOL – Foundation and English for Young Adults – entry 2/3 This class was described as FEYA (Foundation and English for Young Adults 16–21) plus ICT and was directed at learners at Entry 2/3 level. The primary aim was to improve communication and accuracy in writing. This was done by using WebCT (using email, bulletin board, and chat) for communication between two groups of learners. There were 18 learners enrolled on this course, and the usual attendance was about 16. The class lasted one and a half hours.	ESOL (FEYA) – GS2
JP – ESOL – entry 1–3/Level 1 This involved three sessions from three different literacy/ESOL courses conducted by the same lecturer at the same site. The courses were ESOL and ICT (one hour class), ESOL Entry Level 1–3 workshop (two hour class) and Returning to Study: Literacy Entry Level 3/Level 1 (three hour class). In Class 1, ICT was viewed as a tool for teaching. It was used to access the Internet and to access real-time information. In Class 2, ICT was used to support learning in a workshop context. In Class 3, ICT teaching was quite explicit, though the eventual goal was to produce a website to publish the learners' own writing.	ESOL (JP)
CN – literacy – Level 2 This was a literacy course – Level 2. The learners had two sessions with this tutor during the days that sessions were observed. Computers were used only during the afternoon sessions. The morning sessions were used for teaching and the afternoon ICT sessions for practice. The literacy objectives were the primary objectives and ICT was used as a tool for practicing literacy skills. There were 14 learners enrolled on this course, and the usual attendance was about ten.	Literacy – CN

Classess observed and label	Short label

JB – literacy – Level 1

Literacy – JB

This was a Level 1 literacy class. Literacy aims were seen as primary and ICT was used only in so far as it could directly help the achievement of those aims. There were 14 learners enrolled on this course and the usual attendance was about 11. The class lasted two and a half hours.

SG – literacy with PCs – entry 3/Level 1

Literacy – SG

The tutor for this class had both ICT and literacy aims. For example, he was concerned to improve the learners' use of punctuation and their skills in using Word. For most of the time the literacy objectives were seen as primary and the ICT supported those aims. However, there was a clear intention to develop ICT skills as well. There were 12 learners enrolled on this course, and the usual attendance was about eight. The class lasted two hours.

ES1 – free-standing maths unit – Level 2

Numeracy (FSMU) – ES1

This class was a free-standing mathematics unit in a practical Skills course – Level 2. The learners don't stay and so the class had become a form of drop-in facility with individual support. The use of spreadsheets and calculators was a compulsory part of the class and learners were expected to use them in their assignments. The use of spreadsheets and calculators was seen as an aspect of mathematics. There were 18 learners enrolled on this course and the usual attendance was about four or five. The class lasted one and a half hours.

ES2 – GCSE mathematics

Numeracy (GCSE) – ES2

This was a GCSE mathematics class. Some of the students were GCSE repeaters; and others were graduates who required a GCSE grade C to get into a teacher-training course. ICT was used throughout the sessions and was seen primarily as a means of delivering the numeracy content. There were 20 learners enrolled on this course, and the usual attendance was about 12. The class lasted three hours.

JN – numeracy – Level 1

Numeracy – JN

This class was a numeracy Level 1 course. The learning objectives included only numeracy objectives. There was no plan to teach ICT skills and computers were to be used as a way to practice numeracy skills taught in other sessions (usually the day before). There were 22 learners enrolled on this course, and the usual attendance was about 11.

JP – numeracy – entry 1

Numeracy – JP

This was an Entry Level 1 numeracy course. The learners were being introduced to the Internet as a way to access interactive learning materials. There were six learners enrolled on this course, and the usual attendance was about four. The class lasted one hour. In one session the computer system was down.

Findings of the structured observations

In this section we will present the results gathered from the structured observational data, that is, the more quantitative data, first by topic and then by tutor. In interpreting these tables it is necessary to keep in mind how they were generated. The coding is for the predominant category over the previous five minutes; other things may well have been going on during these five minutes. However, these tables do enable a quick overview of the way in which ICT was being used and of the differences in the use of ICT between tutors and between the three areas of literacy, numeracy and ESOL. A more detailed picture can then be generated from the narrative observational accounts and that will be done in the next section.

Results by topic

Table 1 shows the number of observational units for the range of styles of use that were observed. By far the most prominent use of ICT was the interactive use of desktop computers (85 per cent)[9]. Occasionally the desktop machines were used purely as a presentation device; that is, the learner ran a presentation and watched it without any interaction. There was a small amount of use of audio (mainly in one class, which used CD-ROMs that had an audio element). There was some use of data projectors (9 per cent) sometimes with the learners looking and listening and sometimes with them working on their desktop machines. There was no observed use of any other ICT equipment and in particular no use of interactive whiteboards. (There was an interactive white board available in one classroom, but the tutor did not know how to use it.)

Style of ICT use	Total	% of all observations	% where ICT used
Desktop	488	63	85
Desktop with audio	28	4	5
Desktop as presentation device	4	1	1
Projector	26	3	5
Desktop and projector	25	3	4
ICT not predominant	203	26	
	774		

Table 1: Style of ICT use

Table 2 shows the number of observational units for the types of ICT use that were observed. Office software and educational software were the predominant types of ICT use, with a little more use of office software (43 per cent) than educational software (35 per cent). Using the Internet to access information was a significant use, but it was not large (11 per cent) and there was only a small use of communication tools such as email (2 per cent). A surprising amount of time (9 per cent) was spent simply logging on and off – probably a result of both poor user skills and slow networks.

---

9. Percentages quoted in this section will be percentages of the observational units in which ICT was used unless otherwise stated.

Type of ICT use	Total	% of all observations	% where ICT used
Logging on or off	53	7	9
Office software	248	32	43
Educational software	200	26	35
Accessing information	60	8	11
Communication	10	1	2
ICT not predominant	203	26	
	774		

Table 2: Type of ICT use

Table 3 shows the number of observational units for the range of possible users of ICT. The great majority of use (75 per cent) was by individuals working on their own machines. There was only a small amount of use by small groups (10 per cent). Given the emphasis often put on group work in discussion about ICT and learning this is a surprising result. The use of ICT by the tutor with the whole class was very small (2 per cent), which again suggests that certain styles of ICT in teaching were being under exploited. The tutor alone used ICT on 9 per cent of the observational units, these were times where the tutor had to set something up for the learners, but was not directly interacting with the learners whilst doing so.

Users of ICT	Total	% of all observations	% where ICT used
Individual learner	431	56	75
Small group	58	7	10
Tutor and learner	25	3	4
Tutor and small group	2	0	0
Tutor and whole class	12	2	2
Tutor only	43	6	8
ICT not predominant	203	26	
	774		

Table 3: Users of ICT use

Table 4 shows the number of observational units for the range of purposes of ICT use. The main purpose for using ICT was for practice (55 per cent), with a significant, but not large, proportion (15 per cent) devoted to entering information (this was chiefly writing with a word processor and entering data and formulae into spreadsheets) and similar proportions devoted to retrieving information from the Internet (16 per cent) and developing ICT skills (14 per cent). Whilst the use of ICT was often motivating for the learners, only on a very few occasions did the observers feel that ICT was being used purely for motivational reasons.

Purpose of ICT use	Total	% of all observations	% where ICT used
Motivation	8	1	1
Developing ICT skills	78	10	14
Read practice material	15	2	3
Input practice material	295	38	52
Retrieve information	89	11	16
Enter information	86	11	15
ICT not predominant	203	26	
	774		

Table 4: Purpose of ICT use

Table 5 shows the number of observational units for the range of tutor activities that were observed. The tutor spent most time (43 per cent of all observational units) in discussion with individual learners or small groups and another significant amount of time (41 per cent of all observational units) addressing the class as a whole ('talking'). So, the tutor was speaking during 84 per cent of the observational units. The very small amount of time recorded as devoted to listening needs to be interpreted within the context of the way that the observations were conducted, clearly the tutors did much listening while they were discussing and while they were talking, but it was not the predominant activity during that time. Only a small amount of time (7 per cent of all observational units) was devoted to observing learners rather than interacting with them. One tutor in particular saw this as an important teaching activity, but the majority of tutors did not place any emphasis on this activity.

Tutor activity	Total	% of all observations	% where ICT used
Talking	319	41	36
Discussing	334	43	49
Listening	2	0	0
Observing	55	7	8
Reading	13	2	1
Writing	1	0	0
Using ICT	16	2	3
Other task	34	4	3
	774		

Table 5: Tutor activity

Table 6 shows the number of observational units for the range of learner activities that were observed. The learners spent the largest proportion of their time (34 per cent of all observational units) involved in discussion either with the teacher or with other learners and a similar proportion of their time (29 per cent of all observational units) quietly working with the computer. Significant proportions of time were spent in talking and in listening (10 per cent and 16 per cent of all units respectively), but only small amounts in off-screen reading and writing activities (3 per cent and 5 per cent of all units respectively).

Learner activity	Total	% of all observations	% where ICT used
Talking	81	10	5
Discussing	261	34	35
Listening	127	16	14
Reading	24	3	4
Writing	41	5	3
Using ICT	225	29	39
Off task	15	2	0
	774		

Table 6: Learner activity

Table 7 shows the number of observational units for the range of equipment that was seen in use. Whilst unsurprisingly (since this was what we were looking at) ICT was predominant (61 per cent of all observational units), there was significant use of pen and paper for individual work and whiteboards and of large screens for class work (14 per cent and 10 per cent of all observational units respectively). Texts such as handouts were used in 7 per cent of all units, and no equipment at all used in 6 per cent of all units.

Equipment used	Total	% of all observations
ICT	474	61
Board/large screen	81	10
Text/handout	58	7
Pen and paper	109	14
Other	7	1
None	45	6
	774	

Table 7: Equipment used

Table 8 shows the number of observational units where problems occurred. We had anticipated that there might be technical problems associated with the use of ICT in the classroom, and so made particular note of the kinds of problems that occurred in using the technology (see Table 7) and who was affected by them (see Table 8). The tables show that there were relatively few technical problems, in just 4 per cent of observational units in which ICT was being used were technical problems noted. The two main problems that did occur were firstly with the computer network (the usual problem being delays in logging into slow networks) and secondly with printers that did not function. Table 8 somewhat underestimates the degree of technical problems in that the observations for one tutor were delayed by several weeks because of problems with the college computer network and there were two observed sessions where a teacher had changed his/her teaching plans since they knew that the network was down. There were also sometimes technical issues related to the installation of software – tutors commonly reported that they were unable to have new software installed on the college network.

Problems with ICT equipment	Total	% of all observations
None	740	96
Hardware	12	2
Network	17	2
Software	2	0
Other	3	0
	774	

Table 8: Problems with ICT equipment

Table 9 shows that where problems did occur then they tended to affect relatively few learners. However this omits those occasions when there was no attempt to use ICT because of known problems with the computer system.

Users with ICT problem	Total	% of all observations
None	740	96
Whole class	1	0
Individual learner	15	2
Several learners	13	2
Tutor	5	1
	774	

Table 9: Users with ICT problem

Results by classes

In this section we compare the frequencies for the various topics for the 11 classes observed, this enables us to see differences between individual tutors and classes, but more significantly to observe differences between the three areas of ESOL, literacy and numeracy in their use of ICT.

Figure 2 shows that there was greater use of data projectors in the ESOL classes than in the literacy and numeracy classes and that audio was only used in one class – a numeracy class in which the tutor made considerable use of CD-ROMs.

Figure 2: Style of ICT use

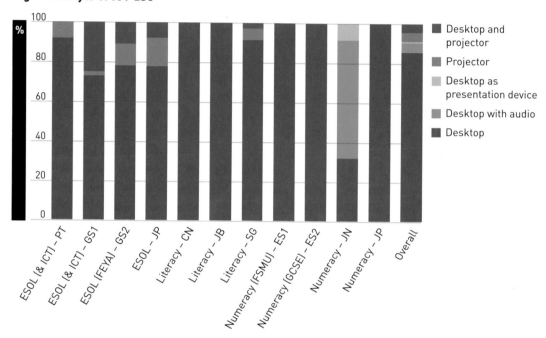

Figure 3 shows greater use of the Internet for accessing information in the ESOL classes than in the literacy and numeracy classes, with one ESOL class making significant use of communications (email). The use of educational software was particularly dominant in the numeracy classes and consequently the use of office software was much less.

Figure 3: Type of ICT use

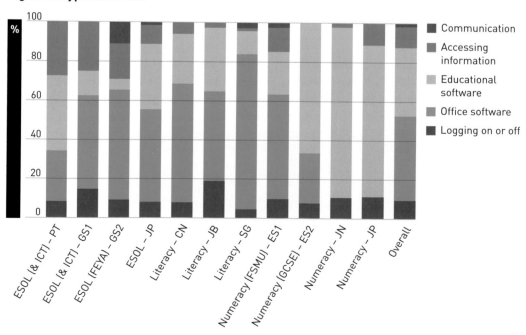

Figure 4 shows significant use of small group work with ICT in the ESOL and literacy classes, with almost none in the numeracy classes. There were also times in the ESOL and literacy classes when the tutor was the sole user of the technology, suggesting a particular style of presentational use of the technology that was not present in the numeracy classes, probably connected with the greater use of data projectors in these classes.

Figure 4: Users of ICT

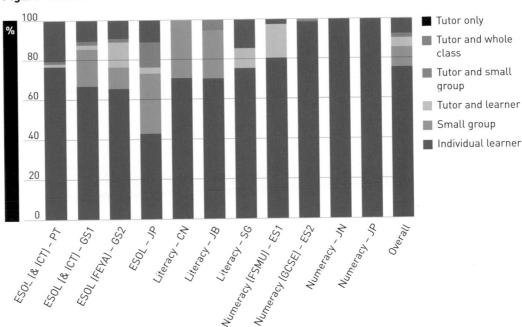

Figure 5 shows that all classes had a mixture of purposes for the use of ICT, with the class ESOL & ICT – GS1 being notable for showing all six identified purposes and the numeracy courses showing the least variety. The modal number of purposes observed was five for the ESOL classes, four for the literacy classes and three and a half for the numeracy classes. One of the numeracy courses had a high proportion for 'enter information' and this relates to the heavy use of spreadsheets for data entry and graph plotting in this class. The amount of use of ICT for practice varies between tutors and to some extent between the three subjects, with the ESOL classes having a little less use of ICT for practice.

Figure 5: Purpose of ICT use

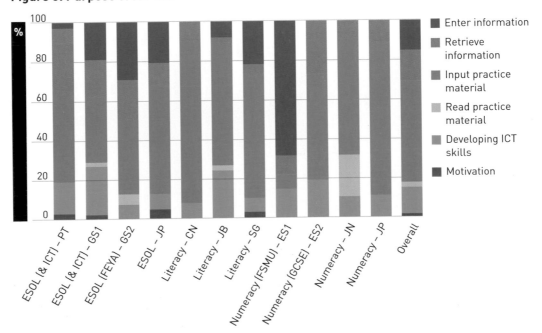

Figure 6 shows some variation between tutors in the balance between talking to the class as a whole and involvement in discussion with individual and small groups. The literacy classes had the lowest level of teacher exposition, but one of the numeracy classes had very low levels of teacher exposition and the majority of work in this class was presented via individual tutorial work. The ESOL classes had quite high levels of the teacher talking.

Figure 6: Tutor activity

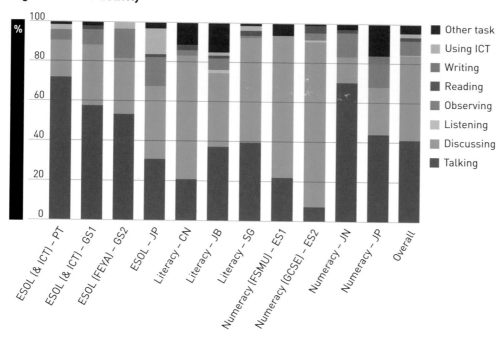

Figure 7 shows variations between classes in the spread of learner activity. Using ICT here indicates the predominant activity as being quiet use of the technology, the low level of this category in some classes is because the class activity was dominated by discussion and talk. The only significant amount of off-task activity was in numeracy classes. The ESOL and literacy classes showed a wider coverage of the six classifications of on-task behaviour than did the numeracy classes: for ESOL the mode was five and a half, for literacy six and for numeracy four.

Figure 7: Learner activity

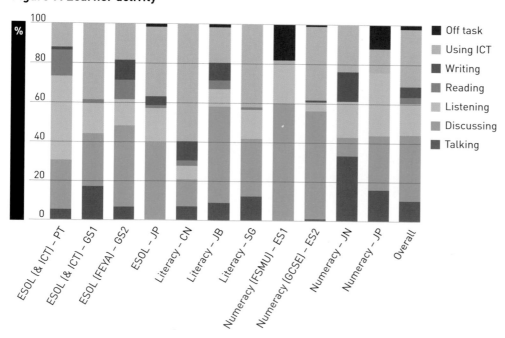

Figure 8 indicates high levels of ICT use in ESOL classes and lower levels in most of the numeracy classes – with the exception of class ES1 – and literacy falling between the two. There were significant levels of the use of pen and paper in the numeracy classes.

Figure 8: Equipment used

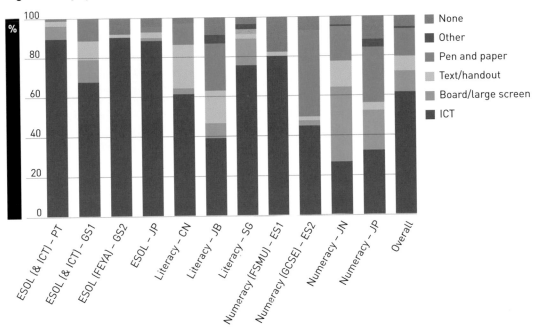

These figures lend some support for the view that individual teachers had their own specific styles of ICT use. Other evidence derived from observations and interviews lends some support to the view that ICT use may relate to personal teaching styles and educational philosophy – this will be discussed later in this report.

These figures above also offer support for the view that there were somewhat different patterns of use in the classes we observed in the three subject areas of ESOL, literacy and numeracy, which are summarised below.

ESOL	Literacy		Numeracy
Style of ICT use	More use of data projectors.		Audio used in one class in which the tutor made considerable use of CD-ROMs.
Type of ICT use	More use of the Internet for accessing information.		More use of educational software.
	One class made significant use of communications (email).		Less use of office software.
Users of ICT	Significant use of small group work.	Significant use of small group work.	Almost no use of small group work.
Purpose of ICT use	High number of purposes (mode 5).	Medium number of purposes (mode 4).	Low number of purposes (mode 3.5).
	Less use of ICT for practice.		

ESOL	Literacy		Numeracy
Tutor activity	More tutor talk.	Less tutor talk.	One of the numeracy classes had very little teacher exposition and the majority of work in this class was presented via individual tutorial work.
Learner activity	Wider coverage of the six classifications of on-task behaviour, (mode 5.5).	Wider coverage of the six classifications of on-task behaviour, (mode 6).	Narrower coverage of the six classifications of on-task behaviour, (mode 4). The only significant amount of off-task activity was in numeracy classes.
Equipment used	High level of ICT use.	Medium level of ICT use.	Relatively low level of ICT use in some classes.

There appears to have been a greater use of a wider range of ICT in ESOL teaching than in most of the literacy and numeracy lessons. It is not possible to tell from such a small sample as to why this might be. One possible hypothesis is that there has been a longer tradition of ICT use in ESOL, perhaps arising from the use of computer assisted language learning in commercial English language teaching institutions. However, equally plausible hypotheses might relate to the training cultures associated with the different groups of tutors, resulting in differing teaching styles, or to the different demands of the subjects being taught.

Addressing the questions

In this section we combine the insights from the narrative aspects of the observational data (that is the more qualitative data summarised in the case studies) with the information from the structured observations presented above and with the information gained from looking at relationships between topics within the structured observations[10]. Specific examples from the case studies are given within the text in order to illustrate the points being made and these extracts are marked in grey.

Curriculum

Relationship of ICT and content objectives

There was a spectrum of integration of ICT with teaching basic skills. At one extreme, ICT was seen as just another teaching tool and the technological demands were kept to a minimum. At the other extreme, ICT skills were seen as important elements of new literacies.

For many tutors the aims of the class were two-fold, taking in literacy, numeracy or ESOL aims together with learning ICT skills. Some tutors talked about the integration of the two sets of objectives, but others talked of ICT being used for consolidation.

Some tutors saw the literacy and numeracy aims as primary and used ICT only in so far as it would directly help the achievement of those aims . For example, one tutor had changed the name of his class from 'ICT and Literacy' to 'Literacy with a PC' to indicate that the emphasis would be on literacy rather than ICT.

In some classes ICT was a part of the curriculum and the learners were expected to use ICT in their assignments, for example the use of spreadsheets in numeracy classes.

In a number of cases the classes were split into separate sessions with one session devoted to classroom teaching and another session to working with ICT – often practising, though sometimes developing and extending, the learning done in the previous class.

Ginsburg (1998) has described four approaches to the use of technology within adult basic skills education as follows.

Technology as curriculum

From the perspective of maximizing the acquisition of information about and competence in using specific technology applications, a curriculum focused on the computer and its applications might be desirable. Components of such a curriculum include keyboarding skills, database manipulation, spreadsheet use, word processing, desktop and Internet publishing, and Internet search skills. Hands-on opportunities to develop a comfort level with the various applications and discussions about the kinds of tasks that might be best managed with each application would provide a basis for using the technology in the various situations in which it is appropriate. Ginsburg (1998) p. 37

---

10. Our immediate aim in addressing these research questions is to gain insights into what was happening within the classrooms we were observing, it is not to make generalisations about what is happening elsewhere. However, our earlier studies have given us a wider context of knowledge about the use of ICT in adult literacy, numeracy and ESOL that does enable us to generate hypotheses about the wider picture based on the present data.

Technology as delivery mechanism

Another way that technology can be used in an adult education environment is as an instructional delivery mechanism. Individualized learning systems (ILS) have been designed to provide instruction and practice in each of the subskills that together forms an entire curriculum. Following an initial placement test, each learner is placed at the particular point in the sequence of programmed lessons that is appropriate for him so he does not have to work at tasks that have already been mastered and will not be given tasks for which he does not display prerequisite knowledge. Each learner's progress is tracked within the system so that a learner can return to the same subskill level at which she was working when she stopped using the system. In addition, the learner is unable to progress from one subskill to another without first achieving some predetermined level of mastery. Individual learners' progress through the series of activities can be reported to an instructor as well as to the learner. Ginsburg (1998) p. 38

Technology as complement to instruction

Some adult education programs conduct traditional classes for adult learners but also make available opportunities for learners to use computers to practice skills addressed in class or extend learning. In some settings the instructor assigns a learner to work on a particular piece of educational software that targets a weak or undeveloped skill area; in other settings, a number of software programs are available and learners can explore and use whatever interests them. Additionally, applications software such as word processing programs or spreadsheets may be available. Ginsburg (1998) p. 39–40

Technology as instructional tool

In this approach, technology is seamlessly integrated into the instructional activities of the class. The primary goals and outcomes of instruction remain the stated goals of a class or program — improving literacy and numeracy skills, progress toward high school completion or another gatekeeping target, or functional skills. The development of technology-related skills is a valued, but secondary, outcome. Just as books, workbooks, a chalk board, and paper are tools that are used as needed within the classroom or to support learning, technology applications are used when they are appropriate. Ginsburg, (1998) p. 41

The diagram below attempts to map the classes we observed against these approaches.

	Technology as curriculum	Technology as delivery mechanism	Technology as complement to instruction	Technology as instructional tool
ESOL (& ICT) – PT			Y	Y
ESOL (& ICT) – GS1	Y			
ESOL (FEYA) – GS2				Y
ESOL – JP	Y			Y
Literacy – CN			Y	Y
Literacy – JB			Y	
Literacy – SG	Y			Y
Numeracy (FSMU) – ES1	Y			Y
Numeracy (GCSE) – ES2			Y	Y
Numeracy – JN			Y	
Numeracy – JP			Y	

Table 10: Approaches to using technology in teaching.

We found that we were not able to allocate most classes completely to one approach or the other, but the exercise does highlight the actual range and mixture of approaches being adopted. We saw no examples of the use of 'technology as the delivery mechanism', though one of the tutors has since gone on to explore the use of an Integrated Learning System[11] and we also know of other sites where this is being done. Our sites were selected because they were thought to be integrating ICT and literacy or numeracy and so, unsurprisingly, the use of 'technology as an instructional tool' was the most common approach. However, a number of tutors saw the use of ICT quite specifically as the source of additional practice material and seemed to be adopting the approach of 'technology as a complement to instruction'. This is an important distinction that tutors incorporating ICT in their classrooms need to address, so that they are clear about their own objectives.

It is also worth noting that the level of ICT skills being developed was often quite low and if we measure them against the proposed levels for ICT as a *Skill for Life*[12] we see that learners were generally working at a lower level in ICT than in literacy or numeracy.

GS1 – ESOL & ICT – entry 3

This is an example of a class in which the tutor adopted the technology as curriculum approach. This was a non-assessed IT option within an ESOL entry Level 3 course. The overall aim of the course was for learners to develop a way of presenting their language work, developing documents in Word, importing them into Front Page and then publishing them as personal websites in WebCT. They were to produce text talking about themselves, their country and their family and to incorporate pictures with their text. The tutor expected that the ESOL learners in this class would be working on topics during their language lessons and that these topics would then form the basis for their personal web pages. This is an ICT class and the ICT learning objectives are the primary objectives. The tutor (who was himself also an ESOL teacher) was aware of the learners' abilities in English and at times he helped them with their English, but ICT aims were his priority.

JN – numeracy – Level 1

This is an example of a class in which the tutor adopted the technology as complement to instruction approach. The learning objectives of this class included only numeracy objectives. There was no plan to teach ICT skills and computers were to be used as a way to practice numeracy skills taught in other sessions (usually the day before). The tutor said that since ICT was not the focus of the class then the ICT demands should be kept to a minimum so that attention was not drawn away from the main purpose of the class. The tutor stressed two particular advantages for using computers: the possibility of visual display (something she had found particularly useful in teaching fractions) and the possibility for learners to work through materials at their own pace and thus to provide the opportunity for exercise and reinforcement. The tutor had spent a lot of time identifying appropriate CD-ROMs ('Numbers You Need' and 'Numbers Disc'[13]) for this course, and in carefully mapping elements of the materials to the topics to be taught. She felt that she needed this time to familiarise herself with the materials, to make sure that they could support her teaching objectives and to make sure that the learners would not need a high level of ICT skills to use the software.

---

11. An Integrated Learning System (ILS) is a computer-based system of teaching, incorporating a program of instruction, and assessment and management tools that provide an individualised programme of study.
12. http://www.qca.org.uk/qualifications/types/2791.html - accessed 18 May 2004
13. These CD-ROMs are both produced by Cambridge Training and Development Ltd (CTAD) – see http://www.ctad.co.uk/home/home.htm - accessed 18 May 2004.

JP – ESOL – entry 1–3/Level 1

The approach adopted by the tutor in this class was harder to classify and incorporated aspects of both the technology as curriculum approach and the technology as instructional tool approach. The tutor had changed the name of this class from 'ICT and Literacy' to 'Literacy with a PC' to indicate that the emphasis would be on literacy rather than ICT, though computers would be frequently used. For most of the time the literacy objectives were seen as primary and the ICT supported those aims. However, there was a clear intention to develop ICT skills as well and learners also welcomed this aspect. For example, in one session one learner made significant use of drawing facilities within Word and other learners wanted to do this as well and so, in the next session the tutor set out to teach the use of the drawing toolbar.

Learning objectives of tutors/learning goals of learners

It was clear that most (though not quite all) learners shared their tutors' concerns to develop ICT skills as well as literacy and numeracy skills and saw this as an important part of the course, something they enjoyed doing and something which they believed would help in the world of work and sometimes at home as well (such as keeping up with their children). Most students seemed to be well motivated and involved, enjoyed the lessons and were able to achieve the lesson objectives.

SG – literacy with PCs – Entry 3/Level 1

The tutor used a short questionnaire to ascertain learners' views about using computers in their learning. It appeared that most learners chose this class because they wanted to improve both their literacy and ICT skills and they enjoyed using computers. Only one of them wrote that she did not really mind if they were using computers or not and one other was not confident in computer use. The learners wanted to learn more about how to use Word and the tutor tried to accommodate their needs.

JN – numeracy – Level 1

In this class, the learners appeared to enjoy working with ICT as a way of learning numeracy. One learner commented that it was the use of visual images that made computers enjoyable and another learner, who was observed to be withdrawn in whole-class teaching, worked with concentration when using the computer. One learner said that the mathematics was too easy for her and that she was only taking this class because of her poor English skills. The software allowed her to work at her own pace, which was clearly faster than the rest of the class, though she still said that she wanted something more challenging.

GS1 – ESOL & ICT – Entry 3

As this was an optional class the learners had chosen this class because they wanted to improve their computer skills. For many students there was a strong match between the tutor's learning objectives and learners' goals. Students observed were attending lessons regularly, able to follow the tutor's instructions and clearly learning computer skills and also enjoying the lessons. However, some learners needed to work at a slower pace and needed more support than the tutor was able to give within the context of this class. For example, one student was observed who was clearly not able to follow the tutor's instructions and did not appear to enjoy the lessons. She needed constant support and guidance by the tutor, something that was impossible to give within the context of the class. (The tutor attributed this student's difficulties to the fact that she was not attending class very regularly and that she did not have time to attend the Learning Centre during the week because of childcare responsibilities.)

Accreditation of ICT as well as literacy and numeracy

In very little of the work we saw was ICT work being accredited and this did not seem to be an issue for learners or tutors. Some tutors actually talked of accreditation as a straight jacket on the ICT work and deliberately avoided it. One of the downsides of this was that we saw little in terms of a structured curriculum for ICT and no explicit assessment of ICT skills. The accreditation of literacy and numeracy work may actually have had some deleterious effects on the way that classes were conducted – seemingly forcing learners to work individually in order to produce their own work for accreditation.

Progression was informally assessed by the tutor's observation of the learners' achievement of the lesson objectives. This informal assessment generally consisted of tutors visiting learners and discussing their work with them, making suggestions for improvement and checking answers. In a number of classes learners were encouraged to print out their work as they went along in order to build up a portfolio.

Several classes ended with the learners devising a record of work, starting from a discussion of what they had learnt in that session. However, the tutors nearly always took control of the discussion and directed learners what to say and what to write.

We saw no use of online assessment in this study.

Difference between ESOL and literacy

We expected to find clear differences between ESOL and literacy classes, but in practice the division between the two was somewhat blurred because the area where the study was carried out had a large immigrant population. However, the analyses of the quantitative data did highlight some differences in the way that ICT was used in the literacy and ESOL classes observed. Tutors in the ESOL classes spent more time talking to the whole class than did those in literacy classes (see Figure 6). In ESOL classes there was a somewhat higher level of use of ICT (see Figure 8), greater use of the data projector (see Figure 2), of the Internet for accessing information and of email (see Figure 3). In literacy classes there was less tutor talk (see Figure 6), somewhat less use of ICT and correspondingly more use of paper-based materials (see Figure 8) and the ICT use was principally the use of desktop machines (see Figure 2) for office software (see Figure 3). So whilst there was not always a very clear division between the two types of classes in terms of student populations, there were differences in the way that ESOL and literacy teachers approached the use of technology within teaching. It was not clear whether this was a conscious choice on the part of the tutor in order to match learner needs, or a reflection of different styles of teaching associated with different subjects.

ICT

How ICT is used

The predominant pattern of activity was for learners to use a desktop computer on their own with the tutor either talking to the whole class, or involved in discussion with groups or individuals. About half of the observed work was with office software and half with educational software. The majority of ICT use was directed towards practice but there was some use related to the creation of new materials and accessing information.

Different types of computer use were associated with different classroom behaviours:

- Office software tended to be associated with individual use of the computer and with the tutor discussing issues with the class, groups or individuals rather than talking to the class as a whole.
- Educational software was associated with learners listening more, discussing less and making more use of pen and paper.
- Accessing information was associated to some extent with the tutor talking, working in groups and with more reading.
- Large screen computer projection was mainly used by the tutor rather than the learners and in all classes where it was used it was connected to the tutor's computer. The projected large screen was most frequently used for the presentation of new material to the whole class.

Examples of educational software included:

- Interactive tutorials for teaching punctuation.
- Exercises on the BBC Skillswise website[14] (such as making simple and compound sentences).
- CD-ROM based numeracy software.

There was widespread use of word-processing for writing and for the construction of language exercises. The internet was widely used for accessing information. For example, in a research project on immigrant populations In Tower Hamlets and to access up-to-the-minute currency rates as part of a numeracy exercise.

Some tutors used ICT to deliver teaching materials to learners:

- One used the college intranet to distribute assignments and the learners did their assignments online.
- Another prepared online presentations and interactive demonstrations that he put on the intranet and directed learners to access them during sessions.
- Another delivered the teaching materials via email and the learners sent in their work via email.

Just one tutor used email for communication between his learners and those in another college.

Excel was used for data handling in numeracy classes.

ES2 – GCSE mathematics
Computers were used throughout the sessions as one of the main tools for delivering the numeracy objectives via online presentations, and interactive programs, and as the main means of processing the data for the data-handling project.

JB – literacy Level 1
Computers were used as another tool for achieving the aims of each lesson:

Learners worked on the Skillswise website, which provided the teaching materials for practising sentence structures (simple and compound).

---

14. http://www.bbc.co.uk/skillswise/ – accessed 18 May 2004

Learners used the thesaurus in Microsoft Word in order to find synonys for a range of adjectives.

Learners used Word to type words into ready made tables.

Learners used Word to type in a letter that they had previously written and to make sure that it had the right format.

JN – numeracy – Level 1

ICT was used as another way of presenting and practising numeracy concepts and afforded learners the opportunity to work individually at their own pace.

JP – ESOL – entry 1–3/Level 1

ICT was used as a tool for accessing and processing information. Learners had to access a currency website to find real-time information and then use the calculator to calculate the percentage change in value since the day before. Then learners had to access another website and note down rates of exchange for certain currencies. Finally learners had to use Excel to construct a graph of these changes.

SG – literacy with PCs – entry 3/Level 1

The tutor used the college intranet to distribute the assignments. Interactive educational software was used to support the teaching of punctuation. Learners were also encouraged to explore the drawing capabilities of Word, just as a (rather playful) activity in its own right.

ICT as a possible barrier

There were occasions when the way that ICT was being used with a class could act as a barrier to learning, these occurred both at the individual level and at the class level. However, in most cases, the ICT tasks the learners were required to do were fairly straightforward and did not overshadow the completion of the work. One tutor specifically chose educational software for its simplicity of use so as to restrict the ICT demands made on learners and hence the risk of ICT acting as a barrier.

Barriers for Individuals

- Some learners had very poor ICT skills (such as could not control the mouse, access the network, or follow instructions to run a program) this held them back whilst other learners were able to progress.

PT - ESOL and ICT Level 1

H did not know what to do. The tutor did not get to her for some time. When he did get to her he helped her to access the first of the websites listed in the worksheet. As soon as the tutor left, H was stuck again and so she approached other learners and asked for their help. They demonstrated what she had to do, but still she was not sure of what to do. Towards the end of the session the tutor gave her a handout that would help her to answer at least the first three questions, H logged off and left.

A had forgotten her password and this delayed her starting the lesson. She did not know what to do and needed support. She constantly asked the learner next to her for directions and they also talked in their mother tongue.

- A student with good level of literacy skills was observed to be unable to progress with an interactive punctuation exercise because she was not able to insert the cursor at the right place. She could not handle the mouse very well and appeared to be afraid to use it. (However, this was an optional class and she may well have chosen this class in order to address her lack of ICT skills).

- Some learners had very good ICT skills and these could be a distraction. In one class a couple of learners spent most of their time decorating their worksheet by inserting borders, drawing shapes, headings, changing colours, etc. rather than completing the assignment.
- Some learners simply did not like using ICT for learning.

ES2-GCSE Mathematics
'I don't learn anything, I like working on paper for maths, and I have a computer at home and like using the computer for writing up my work and for music and games but not this sort of maths'".

Barriers for Classes
- In a literacy class where learners were not very familiar with the use of Word (for example, they were unfamiliar with altering line spacing, fonts, using tabs) learners needed considerable support for their ICT skills in order to complete their literacy task.
- On a number of occasions tutors were seen to give class demonstrations of reasonably complex procedures and then to find that the learners were unable to carry out the necessary ICT procedures necessitating the tutor visiting each learner in turn in order to demonstrate and explain.
- In other classes the skills were not taught to the class, but only presented on an individual basis as needed – this could cause delays and give rise to frustration on the part of the learners.
- In one numeracy class, observers thought that the ICT skills required were very demanding and over shadowed the mathematical tasks being developed and conceptualised.
- In another numeracy class, the learners needed to use Excel, but many were relatively unfamiliar with it and because of the tutorial style of teaching in what was almost a drop-in style workshop, learners had to wait for the tutor to go to them and the workshop became a constant review of technical skills.

ICT as a basic skill – digital literacies
The use of word processing for writing and of the Internet for accessing information were widely accepted, taken for granted, features of ICT that were seen as basic skills needed by all learners.

JB – literacy – Level 1
The tutor recapped the morning's work on adjectives where they had used a thesaurus (in book form) to find synonyms. The tutor introduced the thesaurus in Word and then gathered the class around a machine to demonstrate how to use it.

The tutor asked the class to type into Word a list of the words from their posters, and to find synonyms using the thesaurus. Learners worked on the task, some printed out the work and used paper dictionaries to check the meanings of suggested words. The tutor was walking around, checking, discussing, suggesting and questioning.

Spreadsheets were seen as part of present-day numeracy.

ES1 – free standing maths unit – Level 2
The use of spreadsheets and calculators was a compulsory part of this class, and the learners were expected to use them in their assignments. The use of spreadsheets and

calculators was seen as an aspect of mathematics. The learning objectives for this class included:

locating and selecting data from a supermarket website.
entering a formula into a spreadsheet and calculate unit cost.
filling down.
copying a spreadsheet and modify it.
determining best buys by calculating the unit cost, using a spreadsheet.
stating how they know that their calculated unit costs are sensible/correct.

We saw classes that explicitly addressed the issues around searching the Internet and of interpreting information found on websites.

CN – literacy – Level 2
Learners in this class were carrying out a project researching immigration in Tower Hamlets. The learners had discussed the backgrounds of immigrant groups in Tower Hamlets and they were each assigned the task of finding information about a specific immigrant population.

The tutor reminded learners about the group they needed to find information for (such as Jewish, Bangladeshi etc.) and ran over the kind of information they needed to find (such as (a) why did they come? (b) size of population now (c) type of business and (d) country. She then gave a short introduction to search engines, including giving a brief description of what the Google initial page looks like and what the page of the results might look like. She also talked about appropriate search terms and encouraged learners to use more than one site.

The following descriptions outline the activities of a number of learners, each of whom was observed for 20 minutes during this class:

Learner A logged on quickly, accessed the Internet, went to Google, and entered 'Chinese in London'. He was not happy with the results and so tried different search terms: 'Chinese in Tower Hamlets'. He clicked on the first result, but the page could not be displayed, so he went back to the results page and clicked on similar pages and found what he saw as a 'useful' site. He quickly identified the section that interested him (on Chinese immigrants), he copied it, opened a Word document and pasted it. He then returned to the web page and read further. At this point, the tutor came by and watched what he was doing. She commented that he would not get all the information needed from one page and that he will probably need to look for another web page. She watched him for a while. Learner A copied another part of the text and pasted it into his Word document. He appeared to have good ICT skills. He easily selected the parts of the text that he wanted, right-clicked to select copy and pasted them into his Word document. He changed the fonts and numbered the points that he pasted in.

Learner B had already visited 2–3 sites and printed out some pages. He said that this was the first time that they had used search engines in this class but that he knew how to search because he had done this frequently at home. He liked using computers in classes and took another class in which language and ICT work were combined. He was confident and had good ICT skills and needed little support from the tutor. The initial instructions given by the tutor were enough. He read an article, printed out just those pages that provided the information he was looking for. After printing something he quickly went through the printout, marking relevant parts and underlining words.

Learner C was looking at a number of web pages, going through them and printing some of them out. He appeared to be confident in his use of ICT and said that he enjoyed using computers. He was looking for information on Black Africans and managed to find a few pieces of information, but he was not very pleased with the quality of the information. He said that the tutor told him to go to the library (because 'books are of a better quality'). He intended to go to the library and hoped to find more detailed and useful information there.

Learner D had been in the library, she sat down at the computer. She said that she had not found the library book that she had found to be very useful for her because it discussed Black-African immigrants in the UK generally and did not provide any specific information about Tower Hamlets. She preferred the information she found on the Internet, she was very pleased with the results. She had accessed a number of sites and was able to rapidly identify material she felt was worth more careful reading. She said that she had used search engines before but that she had not been very confident before, but that she had learnt more in this class.

At the end of the session the tutor stopped the learners and re-stated the aims of the lesson: to produce a group report, with each learner writing one section of it. They briefly discussed what the report should be like: factual, using formal language, with a structured layout and incorporating tables and charts.

However, we did not see any explicit recognition of new genres of writing made available by technology.

ICT as a subject in itself – the vocabulary of ICT

Most tutors did not view ICT as a subject in itself but rather as an instructional tool. Many felt that they did not have the training necessary to teach ICT, for example one tutor said: 'I am not an IT person, sometimes the students know more about computers than I do'.

There were some tutors who took the teaching of ICT as a goal in itself and had developed ways of teaching ICT. One tutor laid particular emphasis on the use ICT terminology. The same tutor set the learners the goal of creating their own website and then took this complex and challenging task and broke it down into a series of smaller and more manageable tasks for each lesson.

Talking about a procedure, demonstrating it and then asking the students to try it on their own was the most frequent mode of teaching ICT skills. A minority of tutors encouraged learners to experiment and discover for themselves how the software worked.

Direct teaching of ICT skills was observed in about ten per cent of the observation units, and tended to be associated with learners and tutors talking and discussing and less with the actual use of ICT. ICT skills were commonly taught in both a procedural and didactic way, with some discussion of purposes and applicability, but little discussion of underlying structures. Learners were not generally encouraged to use the help features of software – possibly because these were felt to be difficult to use or because of lack of linguistic competence on the part of ESOL learners.

CN – literacy – Level 2
At the beginning of each session, the tutor explained to learners what they were to do and how they should use the computers, sometimes writing notes, URLs, etc. on the board, but there were no demonstrations of ICT procedures. ICT skills were mostly taught as the tutor

helped learners when they had ICT problems (such as use of arrows, accessing Word, and different ways to 'rub out').

ES1 – free-standing maths unit –Level 2

ICT skills were taught on a one-to-one basis, examples observed included adding titles to columns, creating formulae, typing data, filling in forms, adjusting the width of columns, using the undo function. This might be done by explanation for those with better ICT skills, or by taking over control of the computer and demonstrating the procedure for those with poorer ICT skills.

GS1 – ESOL & ICT – Entry 3

The tutor tended to integrate the use of several pieces of software in order to demonstrate that many of the learners' ICT skills were transferable. He also encouraged the use of ICT terminology and using commands from the keyboard. Learners were asked to perform complex tasks, though these were broken down into simpler sub-tasks.

JN – numeracy – Level 1

The only ICT skills needed in order to use the software chosen for this class were actions of clicking, dragging, typing words and moving forward and backward in the program. These actions were felt to be simple and the tutor did not set out to teach them. The tutor would teach specific ICT skills to individual learners if a problem arose, examples observed included: logging-on, finding the program, navigating the program and increasing the sound level. On one occasion the tutor stopped the class in order to demonstrate how to use the index within the program in order to access specific materials.

SG – literacy with PCs – Entry 3/Level 1

The majority of the learners in this class already had the necessary ICT skills to open and work on Word documents. However, the tutor aimed at improving their ICT skills, such as adding and customising bullet points, customising a paragraph, using spellcheck and using the Draw toolbar. He demonstrated the procedures using the data projector and then talked with learners individually to make sure that they knew what to do.

Technological breakdown

Technological breakdown was less common than we had feared. The main problem lay in the college networks; these occasionally collapsed entirely, but more often caused problems due to slowness, making it difficult to log-on and access resources. Tutors were generally well prepared for the breakdowns that did occur and found ways to work around the problem.

SG – literacy with PCs – Entry 3/Level 1

The tutor came into class before the learners arrived and checked the website needed for the class, discovered that it was unavailable, modified his plans and the lesson was not disrupted. The website became accessible later and so the tutor was able to incorporate this work later in the session.

PT – ESOL & ICT – Level 1

The tutor did not invite us to the college earlier in the year because of technical problems with the college computer system.

In one session it was observed the computer system was very slow. It took learners a great deal of time to log-on and to access the Internet or open a Word document (for example, one learner was not able to start working until 50 minutes after the session began). Learners were frustrated and unsure of what they should do because they did not know whether it was the system's fault or whether they had done something wrong themselves.

On another occasion the tutor had requested a laptop for the introduction of the session. The technician was almost an hour late in delivering it and thus the tutor could not use it as planned. The lesson plan read: 'Set scene. SS have just moved to borough; they have a family with two small children and want to find out more about what it has to offer. What sort of things would they want to know?'. The tutor was unable to set out this imaginary scene for the learners and so they were unsure why they were searching for specific information. When the tutor tried to use the laptop, he found that it was not connected to the Internet and therefore he could not demonstrate how to access the websites he wished them to use.

Learners

Learning preferences

One of the claimed benefits of ICT use in learning is the possibility of adapting to individual learning preferences. The visual elements of ICT presentation were useful to many learners and for others the ability to adapt to their pace of work was important and these will be important issues for us to examine in future work when we look more closely at the learners experience. However, in looking at what tutors were doing we saw few attempts by tutors to accommodate students' learning styles in other ways.

Some learners clearly preferred working with ICT to other forms of learning. One learner who rarely participated in class activities would work with concentration on the computer. Dyslexic learners often preferred using a computer to writing by hand, because it produced neater text, and because of the spell checking facility.

Some learners (perhaps mainly younger learners) were willing to try things out and learn by trial and error rather than wait for the tutor's instructions.

Individual and collaborative working

Working in small groups was observed in less than ten per cent of the observational units. Where learners were working in small groups with ICT they were a little less likely to be using office software and more likely to be using educational software or accessing information than when they were working individually. Unsurprisingly, the use of audio tended to concentrate even more on individual work – there was less discussion with other learners or teachers and more use of pen and paper. This reflects the fact that the only use of audio seen was with educational software and involved the use of earphones.

Learners were generally expected to work individually and achieve the tasks set. Assessment methods, particularly in terms of producing individual coursework or portfolios, tended to encourage this way of working. However, they were generally free to co-operate and frequent interactions among learners were observed, though in one class in which there were big differences in the literacy skills of the learners, the tutor discouraged those with better literacy skills from helping the others, as they tended to do the work for them.

Paired work on the computers happened often due to the lack of computers for individual work and when additional machines became available most learners chose to work individually.

Whilst individual and whole-group work were the dominant styles, small-group work was encouraged in some literacy and ESOL classes. Only one tutor was observed to structure small-group work – assigning specific roles to each member of the group. For this tutor, peer collaboration was seen as a step towards greater learner autonomy.

GS1 – ESOL & ICT – Entry 3
In one session learners worked in pairs for most of the time, the tutor having assigned the pairs and the role of each member of the pair. During the other three sessions the learners were instructed to work individually; they had to create their own personal web page and each one needed to create their own documents and web pages. However, learners were free to interact with others and ask for their help when the tutor was with another learner. The tutor said that he felt restricted in his use of group work by the room layout, which made it difficult for re-forming groups and for the tutor to circulate and by the fact that learners were facing the machines, which was not conducive to collaboration.

JB – literacy – Level 1
A lot of time was spent as a whole class engaged in discussion with the tutor. However most of the ICT work was done working individually, though sometimes in small groups.

JN – numeracy – Level 1
In this class, learners worked on their own. The class was very quiet and there were only a few interactions among learners principally about maths problems or navigating the software.

SG – literacy with PCs – Entry 3/Level 1
In this class, learners were encouraged to work individually because their assignments would be used for their accreditation. However, there was a very friendly classroom climate and learners frequently asked for the tutor's help. When the tutor was with a learner, other learners who needed help took the initiative to approach the person sitting next to them and asked for help. Learners were asked to work in pairs or trios only in one session, when they were asked to read each other's work and on another occasion were organised into two teams for a competition.

CN – literacy – Level 2
In the main learners worked individually in this class because they had to produce work for accreditation, but they were left free to interact with others or work in pairs, if they preferred to co-operate. In one session the tutor suggested that less ICT-skilled learners should pair up with more skilled learners. Six learners chose to work in pairs and three chose to work individually. There was lots of discussion not only within pairs but also across the whole class. Paired work on the computers was mainly due to the lack of computers for individual work, and when the adjacent classroom became available, most learners chose to work individually.

Feedback
The most frequent feedback was that provided by tutors as they moved around the class talking to individual learners and small groups. Assignments were often collected at the end of classes and homework collected, marked and returned. There was some feedback from peers but this seemed not to be integrated within the pedagogy.

Feedback from ICT materials was positively received by learners, and it enabled learners to work at their own pace. The feedback was usually perceived as useful, but this applied mainly to situations where learners were involved in practising work they knew quite well. When learners were dealing with topics that they did not understand well then computer feedback was much less helpful. There was evidence that some learners were encouraged by feedback to repeat exercises in order to improve their scores, but this could degenerate into a pursuit of getting full marks that could actually be at the cost of understanding what they were doing.

JN – numeracy – Level 1

The software used in these sessions provided immediate feedback to the learners and learners would repeat an exercise if they got it wrong. This often allowed learners to work at their own pace particularly when they were practicing topics that they understood, but where learners were dealing with topics that they did not understand then the feedback was not helpful.

JP – numeracy – Entry 1

The learners received feedback that gave them an explanation of what they might have done wrong. Learners also had the chance to have another go at the questions before trying a different level and they could also receive a 'certificate' that included their results and a general comment. For one learner in particular the feedback received was seen to be very important. She was pleased with her results and with the fact that she could work at a faster rate than others, she did not have to ask the tutor to see her work before moving on. Another learner got eight out of ten questions correct and he was able to see, because of the explanations given, what he had done wrong, realised that these were silly mistakes and that he actually knew how to do these questions and he felt that he did not have to repeat them.

SG – literacy with PCs – Entry 3/Level 1

Learners received instructional feedback when using 'Issues in English'[15]. It appeared that it was very important for them to get a high mark and for at least one learner observed, only a completely correct mark was felt to be satisfactory. Because the learner wanted to get a full mark, she repeated the exercise many times until she succeeded. The tutor said that he was reluctant to use software that provided feedback to learners, as he was concerned that learners' desire for full marks would not necessarily mean that they would learn more or better.

Literacy level of the learners

One group of learners with low levels of oral skills in English was observed and they were able to work on the computer despite their limited English skills and indeed this offered a good way into literacy for them.

Poor literacy levels did not constitute a barrier to the use of ICT in most classes. However, this is partly because the level of ICT skills called on was very limited. Poor literacy levels did form a barrier when accessing online materials (for example making judgements about useful websites to visit) and in understanding ICT terminology (for example when using WebCT or Excel).

CN – literacy – Level 2

In using search engines to obtain information about immigrants the learners came across lots of information, but because of their high level of literacy skills (level 2) they were able to quickly decide whether the information presented was useful or not.

---

15. Published by Protea Textware – see http://www.proteatextware.com.au/english.htm – accessed 18 May 2004

Occasionally the low level of ICT skills of students impacted on their ability to achieve literacy or numeracy goals.

CN – literacy – Level 2
In general learners were able to achieve the tasks set by the tutor and learners did not appear to be frequently stuck because of their ICT skills. Some learners had better ICT skills than others and learners would ask for support from their classmates or their tutor. However, there was one learner with a low level of ICT skills who was frequently stuck and needed support with both her literacy skills and ICT skills.

SG – literacy with PCs – Entry 3/Level 1
There were two incidents where ICT skill levels interacted with the learning of literacy. Two learners with a high level of ICT skills spent much of one session in decorating their assignment sheet by inserting borders, drawing shapes, headings, changing colours, etc. rather than in completing the assignment. Another learner with a high level of literacy skills but poor ICT skills was stuck when using 'Issues in English' because she was not able to insert the cursor and add the punctuation mark where she wanted to put it.

The goals in the following example are mainly ICT goals and a student with good literacy skills finds herself disadvantaged in a more visual rather than textual context.

SG – literacy with PCs – Entry 3/Level 1
In the second part of the lesson the tutor directed the learners to a Word document with instructions for drawing shapes in Word. The tutor demonstrated the Draw toolbar. Most learners repeated what the tutor was doing but one learner could not keep up with the tutor's instructions. This learner had good literacy skills but struggled with the ICT skills. The drawing work was particularly difficult for her because she could not derive any support from her literacy skills. Too much information was presented in too short a time for her and she was completely lost. She could not handle the mouse very skilfully and much of the time she could not click where she wanted to. The worksheet provided did not give instructions as to what the learners were to do, but rather introduced some of the drawing functions and suggested that the learners explore. This learner did not enjoy the exercise.

Learners with low levels of literacy skills sometimes had problems with completing numeracy tasks.

ES1 – free-standing maths unit – Level 2
The literacy level of the learners was quite low and they had problems with completing the numeracy tasks because they had to explain their actions and choices in writing. The tutor needed to spend quite a lot of time helping them to write these explanations. When one learner tried to use the spellcheck in Excel, the tutor suggested that it would not help him very much and instead spelt out the word for him.

Specific characteristics of THIS audience (adults/basic skills)
In the main, classes dealt with themes likely to be of interest to adults, such as preparation for the world of work, for example writing formal letters for job applications.

CN – literacy – Level 2
When most learners finished, the tutor addressed the whole class and introduced the second part of the lesson; finding information from the Internet. The learners were doing research for

a project on immigration patterns in Tower Hamlets. The tutor wrote up the URLs for some search engines, then circulated in class and talked to learners about how they could get the information they needed for the work they were writing.

This session was part of an ongoing project on research about immigration in Tower Hamlets. The learners had discussed the backgrounds of immigrant groups in Tower Hamlets and they were each assigned the task of finding information about a specific immigrant population.

JB – literacy – Level 1
The tutor reviewed the morning lesson on proof reading. She then distributed a handout illustrating the format of a formal letter that they were to follow. Learners read and discussed this with the tutor.

The tutor gathered the class around a computer and demonstrated how to use the text alignment boxes, the tab key, and how to alter spacing and font size. Learners worked on their letters individually, on computers. The tutor circulated discussing learners' work on an individual basis. As they finished the letters, the tutor read them, made suggestions and praised them.

Examples of using ICT materials initially designed for children were seen on a number of occasions and appeared to cause no difficulties.

JN – numeracy – Level 1
The main software being used was 'Numbers you need' from CTAD, originally developed for 10–15 year olds (Key Stages 3–4), but the tutor said that there had been no problems in using it with this group and they did not feel that it was 'childish'.

Teachers

Relation of ICT to teacher style
Most teaching consisted of group presentation followed by an activity supported by individual tutoring, though some sessions consisted exclusively of individual tutoring. The tutors spent about half their time talking to the class as a whole and about half talking with small groups and individuals. The amount of time devoted by tutors to quiet observation of learners was quite small. On some occasions however, tutors sat back and avoided intervening as part of a conscious process of encouraging student independence and autonomy.

The amount of time devoted to the tutors talking was related to the ongoing activities:

- The tutors tended to address the whole class rather than be involved in discussion when learners were using ICT to access information, or developing or practising ICT skills (including logging in or out of the network).
- The tutors tended to be involved in discussion rather than addressing the whole class when learners were entering information, or when using office software.
- When educational software was being used there was a fairly even balance between discussion and talking to the whole class.

In over 85 per cent of the units recorded the tutor was either talking to the class as a whole, or discussing issues with the class, groups or individuals. The balance between these activities was affected by whether ICT was being used or not and by the use of a data

Figure 9: Tutor activity and ICT use

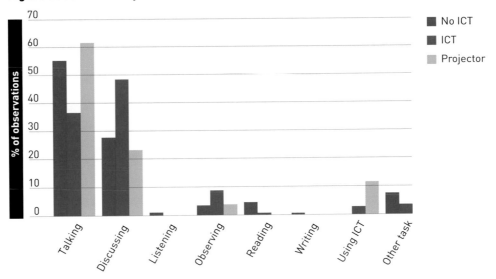

projector. Figure 9 shows that tutors talked to the class less when ICT was being used than when it was not, but that they talked more when using a data projector. The patterns for discussion with learners were the reverse of this.

Figure 10: Learner activity and ICT use

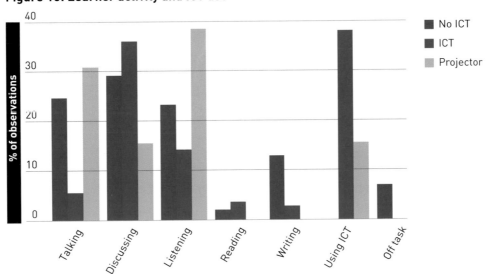

Figure 10 shows that the use of ICT was associated with learners in discussion and that the use of the data projector resulted in periods of listening and of learners talking to the whole class.

Teachers adapted the use of ICT to their own style of teaching. Different patterns of ICT use were found in numeracy, literacy and ESOL. The tutors' level of ICT skills had an impact on their ability to make effective use of the technology. It was also true that specific characteristics of certain technologies affected the way in which these were used in the classroom.

■ We have adopted a number of approaches in order to think about the way that the tutors viewed the task of teaching, what we might loosely call 'teacher style':

- Perspectives – using a classification of perspectives on teaching proposed by Pratt (1998). Perspectives relate to the tutor's philosophy about pedagogy and this is best determined by talking to tutors. Whilst we did not set out specifically to probe tutor's perspectives on teaching, we believe that we have sufficient evidence based on interviews with the tutors, discussions in the workshops and tutors' lesson plans to be able to make a reasonable estimate of the tutors' perspective on teaching.
- Orientation – based on an approach proposed by Askew et al., (1997) and derived from both observational data and discussion with the tutors.
- Task presentation – derived from a reading of the classroom observational data.
- Strategies of ICT use – derived from tutors' lesson plans and from a reading of the classroom observational data.
- Classroom management approaches – derived from a reading of the classroom observational data.

Perspectives

We tried to classify tutors' perspectives according to Pratt's classification (Pratt 1998). For an account of these perspectives see Appendix 2.

i　The Transmission Perspective: Effective Delivery of Content.
ii　The Apprenticeship Perspective: Modelling Ways of Being.
iii　The Developmental Perspective: Cultivating Ways of Thinking.
iv　The Nurturing Perspective: Facilitating Self-efficacy.
v　The Social Reform Perspective: Seeking a Better Society.

The table below indicates our perceptions of the tutors' perspectives – though it is possible that the tutors themselves might have different opinions of their own perspectives. Most of the tutors adopted the transmission perspective, with a number of tutors adopting the apprenticeship perspective. It is interesting that we saw no evidence of tutors adopting the social reform perspective.

Whilst tutors who held the apprenticeship and nurturing perspectives might modify their practice in specific ways in order to accord with their view of teaching, those who held the transmission perspective were in the majority, but they employed a range of different strategies in order to achieve their objectives.

	Transmission	Apprenticeship	Developmental	Nurturing	Social reform
ESOL (& ICT) – PT	Y				
ESOL (& ICT) – GS1	Y				
ESOL (FEYA) – GS2			Y		
ESOL – JP	Y				
Literacy – CN	Y				
Literacy – JB	Y				
Literacy – SG	Y				
Numeracy (FSMU) – ES1		Y		Y	
Numeracy (GCSE) – ES2		Y		Y	
Numeracy – JN	Y				
Numeracy – JP	Y			Y	

Table 11: Perspectives on teaching

Orientation

Askew et al., (1997) have developed an account of three orientations adopted by teachers of numeracy in primary schools:

- *Connectionist* teachers, who were highly effective, concentrated on assisting pupils to develop efficient conceptually based strategies and in doing this used discussion and challenge to introduce links between different meanings and representations.
- *Transmission* teachers, who were only moderately effective, emphasised pupils' acquisition of a set of standard methods for solving a limited range of routine problems, by demonstrating specific methods and ensuring that pupils practiced them.
- *Discovery* teachers, who were only moderately effective, emphasised pupils' known development of concepts and strategies, using practical activities and experience provided by the teacher as a basis. (Askew et al., (1997) p. 48)

No teacher or tutor is likely to adopt any one of these orientations exclusively, but these orientations have some interesting points of resonance with what we saw in the classes that we observed. Since we will already be stretching the concept of these orientations beyond primary education to adult education, we will not seek to stretch it even further to include literacy but will simply give some indications as to aspects of these orientations that we saw in the teaching of numeracy, how this interacted with ICT use and how tutors adapted their use of ICT to fit with their orientation to teaching.

We are not able in this study to provide indications as to how effective these orientations were, though we note that Askew and his colleagues argue strongly for the effectiveness of the connectionist orientation within the context of primary education and that this is something that clearly needs to be explored in the area of adult education.

In a teaching style that might otherwise have been thought to be rather transmissive, the following tutor was seen to be very keen to establish connections between different mathematical representations and between the use of the computer, paper and pencil and mental methods. This tutor had managed to integrate a rather straightforward transmissive CD-ROM training package into a much richer teaching structure.

JN – numeracy – Level 1
The tutor asked all learners to find the 'Numbers You Need' CD-ROM. The learners watched a slide show and the tutor then asked them to explain what it was about. She then related this to the work written on the board. The learners watched other slide shows and discussed them with the tutor, the tutor making connections with data on the whiteboard and the number line.

The tutor had strong control of what happened in the class. She worked systematically through a series of tasks leading to content mastery: she provided clear objectives at the beginning of each session, she expected learners to learn specific things in a specific way, she constantly revised and connected concepts together (e.g., decimals to fractions, to percentages, to the number line), she provided many examples of the same point until she was sure that every learner had understood, she provided help and feedback and at the end of each session she briefly summarised what had been learnt.

Concepts were taught for the first time in non-ICT sessions. The tutor started each ICT session by revising concepts learnt earlier and then she worked through several examples of what had been presented during the last non-ICT session, with the learners proposing possible answers and the class discussing these answers. She demanded active participation by everyone and if a learner was not participating then she would call on them by name. The tutor asked the learners to work on specific sections of the software and to take notes on paper.

This next tutor might be seen as having been primarily transmissive in orientation in her use of ICT in teaching. She directed the learners to the BBC Skillswise website, which was then used for practice exercises.

JP – numeracy – Entry 1

The tutor had clear objectives, which included both numeracy and ICT skills, and tried to take learners systematically through tasks leading to content mastery. She was also aware of the learners' variety of skills, tried to accommodate these and offered learning activities that would be useful and relevant to learners' lives.

The tutor first addressed the whole class before going to the ICT centre, the learners were able to choose what they would like to do (from the BBC Skillswise website) which offered them opportunities to practice their maths skills, the learners worked individually and the tutor walked around and offered support.

Our third example is perhaps closest to the discovery orientation and makes use of both tutor-prepared ICT presentations and open-ended software packages (such as Excel) to allow the learners greater independence.

ES2 – GCSE mathematics

The tutor believed that learners needed to work at their own pace and that they needed to be in control of their rate of learning. The tutor wished to develop learners' autonomy. The use of ICT enabled a greater degree of learner independence. This was evidenced in the sessions observed, but it was also evidenced in this tutor's report of his observation of another tutor's session. In this report one can see which issues were important for him. Here is a part of this report:

> "I was not convinced that the students were learning, they were largely able to complete the tasks without too much trouble having already understood the topic from what have been previously taught. There was no differentiation as all students did the same tasks. There was no accommodation for preferred learning styles. I did not think there was evidence of student autonomy in the control of their rate of learning."

The tutor worked individually with the learners and rarely did he have whole-class teaching. Commonly, task instructions were given through discussion with individual learners rather than by a presentation to the whole class. He often spent a considerable time with each learner in order to explain and go through the task. He had created online teaching materials for the college intranet that allowed learners to go through presentations and activities at their own pace.

Task presentation

The following outlines the approaches taken by each of the tutors to the presentation of tasks.

GS The tutor worked systematically through a series of tasks leading to content mastery, providing clear objectives at the beginning of each session.

A common method was to demonstrate what the learners had to do and to use closed type questions during the demonstration to ensure that learners understood. He frequently asked the learners as a group to repeat what he had just demonstrated. Alternative ways of delivering task instructions were to provide written instructions on worksheets or to direct learners to the location of instructions on the network. He would then circulate in class helping learners individually or in pairs, while continuously providing help and feedback on what learners were doing and then at the end of each session he would summarise what had been done. (The tutor self-deprecatingly described his teaching method as 'Demonstrate and pray'.)

JP The tutor first addressed the whole class, informing them of the session's aims and perhaps giving out a worksheet before going to the IT centre.

The tutor had clear objectives, which included both numeracy and ICT skills and tried to take learners systematically through tasks leading to content mastery. She was also aware of the learners' variety of skills, tried to accommodate these and offered learning activities that would be useful and relevant to learners' lives.

PT The tutor always introduced tasks by clearly describing them in a whole class presentation and then summarising the procedures at the end of the presentation. When task instructions were given, learners were usually either gathered around the tutor's desktop machine or the laptop connected to the data projector, which projected onto the side of the room. The tutor did not provide handouts with the procedures written down but did direct learners to online resources with these instructions. The tutor circulated and helped individuals.

CN The tutor gave the task instructions at the beginning of each session and then got learners to start working. She then visited each individual and made sure that they were working on task.

JB The task instructions were carefully presented and sometimes given as a handout as well. At the beginning of each lesson the tutor set out the lesson's aims and encouraged a discussion around the aims and then gave clear detailed task instructions, always checking that these had been understood before the learners began work. She encouraged class participation through questioning and looking for an answer from each person. She used a range of means to motivate learners and maintain a high level of engagement – posters, cards, OHP, handouts, and computers. ICT was just one of these means and she was able to assimilate their use to her normal teaching style.

SG The tutor talked to the class about the work for the session, offered examples on the board and then showed them where they could find the assignments on the network. The learners were working mainly on their own and the tutor would check with them that they had understood the instructions.

ES The tutor had a tutorial style of teaching: he gave task instructions individually to learners. When a learner came in, he or she was asked to log-on and directed to the task. No presentation device was used for whole-class presentations.

JN The tutor worked systematically through a series of tasks leading to content mastery: she provided clear objectives at the beginning of each session, expected learners to learn specific things in a specific way, constantly revised and connected concepts together (such as decimals to fractions to percentages to number line), provided many examples of the same point until she was sure that every learner had understood, provided help and feedback, and at the end of each session briefly summarised what had been learnt.

Concepts were taught for the first time in non-ICT sessions. The tutor started each ICT session by revising concepts learnt earlier and then she worked through several examples of what had been presented during the last non-ICT session, with the learners proposing possible answers and the class discussing these answers.

Teaching strategies

We can classify the actual observed use of ICT-based teaching strategies into two categories, that align fairly well with the two approaches to the use of technology that Ginsburg (1998) labels as 'Technology as instructional tool' and 'Technology as complement to instruction'.

■ ICT used as the main way of teaching.
This approach might be used to teach either literacy or numeracy or ICT skills:

- Literacy or numeracy – GS used ICT as the main tool for teaching and it was used throughout all sessions. The teaching materials were often delivered to learners via email and learners also sent in their work via email. The purpose was to stimulate the development of ICT skills necessary for communication (such as receiving an email invitation, replying, inviting people).
- ICT skills – ES taught the use of Excel through interactive exercises and through the use of Excel for data handling tasks.

■ ICT was used as one element of the lesson.
- To practice literacy, numeracy or ESOL skills – SG used interactive punctuation exercises to consolidate work on punctuation.
- To present concepts through another medium – JN used the visual presentation features of ICT, a CD-ROM as another tool for presenting difficult numeracy concepts.
- To introduce ideas in a different way – CN developed written work on immigration through Internet searches.
- To motivate learners – JP used a variety of different means (including posters, cards, OHP, handouts, and computers) to motivate learners and maintain a high level of engagement.

Classroom management

Tutors had taken different approaches to managing the use of ICT in the classroom, for some it meant strong central control and careful targeting of resources, for others it meant releasing much more control over the classroom. (This account necessarily has overlaps with the previous section on task presentation, but tries also to bring out the specific classroom management issues that go beyond task presentation.)

GS At the beginning of each lesson the tutor provided learners with the objectives of the
Strong lesson, and demonstrated what he wanted them to do. When he wanted to introduce
control another activity, he would encourage learners to finish quickly what they were doing, check their work and then introduce the next task. Whilst the learners worked on the tasks individually or in small groups the tutor provided support, questioning them, correcting errors in their writing, making suggestions for improvement, directing them

to appropriate resources, helping with ICT problems and emphasising the need to pay attention to the instructions given.

Transitions to and from using the computers were made smoothly by the tutor raising his voice to get attention, sometimes asking learners to turn off their screens, putting a screen image on the projector and drawing the learners' attention to it. The tutor said that he would have liked to have (more!) control over the learners' monitors so that he could blank them out when he wanted to get everyone's attention

The tutor set out to develop the learners' autonomy, and as they became more independent learners his role changed; he offered fewer directions and gave more responsibility to learners to complete tasks on their own. He encouraged learners to support each other and offer appropriate help.

JN Strong control	The tutor provided clear objectives at the beginning of each session, Concepts were taught for the first time in non-ICT sessions. The tutor started each ICT session by revising concepts learnt earlier, and involving the group in solving problems. She expected active participation by everyone. The tutor asked the learners to work on specific sections of the software and to take notes on paper. The learners worked individually on the computers and there were few interactions among them. She constantly revised and connected concepts together (such as decimals to fractions to percentages to number line), provided many examples of the same point until she was sure that every learner had understood, provided help and feedback and at the end of each session briefly summarised what had been learnt.
JB Strong control	At the beginning of each lesson the tutor set out the lesson's aims and encouraged a discussion around the aims. The task instructions were detailed and sometimes given as a handout as well. She checked that the instructions had been understood before the learners began work. She encouraged class participation through questioning and looking for an answer from each person. She used a range of means to motivate learners and maintain a high level of engagement – posters, cards, OHP, handouts and ICT.
PT Medium control	The tutor always introduced tasks by describing them in a whole-class presentation and then summarising the procedures at the end of the presentation. When task instructions were given, learners were usually either gathered around the tutor's desktop machine or the laptop connected to the data projector, which projected on the side of the room. Transitions to and from using computers were not made very smoothly because learners had to leave their seats and because of the large number of students. Because they were out of their places during the demonstrations learners were not able to practice procedures whilst they were being demonstrated and were not able to take notes. The tutor did not provide handouts with the procedures written down, but directed learners to online documents containing these instructions. The tutor circulated and helped individuals, but he needed to spend a significant time with each learner and so learners often had to rely on other learners for help.
CN Medium control	The tutor gave the task instructions at the beginning of each session and then got learners to start working. Initially the learners sat at desks in the centre of the classroom and then moved to the computers that were placed around the walls. The

transition between whole-class discussion and ICT use was done smoothly. As the learners were working on computers, the tutor went round the class, making sure that they were working on task, making suggestions and solving any language or ICT problems. The pace of the lesson was determined by the learners in that the tutor ensured that they had completed the task before moving on. Learners were free to choose how to work (paper work or computer work, pairs or individuals), they were free to choose what task to do first, and they were free to interact frequently with each other and help/support each other.

SG Medium control	When the learners came in they tended to log-in to the network, so the tutor always used an icebreaker activity in order to gain their attention and to draw them away from the computers so that he could introduce the lesson aims to the whole class. He put up examples on the board and then showed them where they could find the assignments on the network. Learners were free to ask for help (from the tutor or other learners), but they were expected to work on task and to produce individual work. The tutor circulated to ensure that they had understood the instructions
JP Light control	The tutor informed learners of the session's aims, and then gave out a worksheet, setting out the tasks to be done. The learners then went to the ICT centre and worked through the worksheet instructions calling on the tutor for additional guidance as required. In some other observed sessions this tutor allowed learners a choice of online activities. Learners were expected to work individually but they frequently interacted, and the tutor walked around and offered support
ES Light control	This class had poor student attendance and punctuality. No presentation device was used and only rarely was there any whole-class teaching. As learners came in, the tutor asked them to log-on and directed them to a task. Sometimes this was an online presentation or interactive exercise that he had prepared on the college intranet. This allowed learners to go through presentations and activities at their own speed. The tutor believed that learners needed to be in control of their rate of learning. The tutor gave task instructions individually to learners and he often spent a considerable time with each learner in order to explain the whole task. Learners were keen to use computers but they were reluctant to experiment and so would often wait for the tutor's help. Learners often had to wait a long time for help because the tutor was engaged with another learner.

Meta-language of the classroom

There was a level of language use used in the classroom about the organisation and structure of the lessons that was at a different level from that of the lessons themselves. This was particularly the case where ICT terminology was needed in order to explain procedures. We did not succeed in capturing sufficient data on this to be able to comment further.

Management of open learning

We did not see enough examples of open learning to be able to provide evidence about this here. Other studies that we have carried out for Ufi/**learndirect** have provided evidence related to one particular form of open learning (Kambouri, Mellar et al., 2003, and Kambouri, Schott et al., 2003)

Recommendations

Recommendations for practice

Observed good practice

We saw a range of what appeared to us to be good practice in the use of ICT in adult literacy and numeracy and we list here the main points that came from our observations.

- Clear lesson aims, explained and/or negotiated with learners at the start of the session, coupled with a review of what has been learnt at the end of the session. (Whilst perhaps always good practice, this has particular importance in directing the learners' attention to what they are expected to learn from the use of the technology and how they are expected to do this).
- A combination of multiple ways of providing information: demonstration through a data projector, handouts and materials stored on the computer network.
- Providing opportunities for peer learning both through small group work and through projection of learners' work for class discussion.
- Flexibility in classroom management terms: accepting collaboration when it occurs naturally, directing learners to specific reinforcement activities if necessary and sometime avoiding intervention as part of a process of encouraging student independence and autonomy.
- For classes adopting the 'instructional tool' approach – a close integration of literacy and numeracy learning objectives with ICT learning objectives and use of technology in a wide variety of ways throughout the session.
- For classes adopting the 'complement to instruction approach' – careful preparation of materials and thorough familiarisation with teaching materials (both those that will be used and those that might be used) before using them with learners. Consolidation of learning through doing the same tasks with and without ICT.

Areas for development
Approaches to using technology
- Tutors need to reflect on why they are using ICT and to match the way that they use the technology to their aims. Ginsburg's (1998) discussion of the range of approaches to using technology in basic skills education may be useful here.
- Teaching also needs to address the changing nature of literacies in the digital age, new types of relationships between media are being created and new genres of writing are developing.

Teaching
- A wider range of technologies and ways of using them needs to be explored. For example, we saw no use of interactive whiteboards. All use that we saw of data-projectors were tutor controlled, we saw no examples of learners taking control of projectors. Digital cameras, digital video, PDAs, mobile phones are just some of the other technologies that could be explored. A wider range of software should be explored – there is much useful practice in schools that could suggest possibilities[16].
- Greater experimentation with teaching styles and forms of classroom management should be encouraged. Does a highly structured approach encourage dependence? Does too loosely structured an approach run the risk of learner frustration?

---

16. The next phase of our work within NRDC (which is already underway) is exploring this range of issues related to effective teaching.

- How do we stop ICT getting in the way of learning? How do we identify learners' ICT skills and find effective methods of teaching ICT skills (whether class teaching, peer learning, effective support materials) that would teach ICT skills without the inefficiency of teaching skills to individual learners.
- Greater attention needs to be given to the range of learning styles and learner preferences and ways in which ICT might be used to address these.

Collaboration

- Work is needed to develop appropriate ways of learners working effectively together using ICT. This needs to go beyond allowing learners to work together towards defining structures and roles for collaborative work. How do we prevent the requirements of assessment getting in the way of the development of collaborative work?

Teaching ICT

- The issue of how to teach ICT needs to be addressed more explicitly. Tutors who adopt a wider range of strategies for developing learners' literacy and numeracy skills sometimes adopt a purely didactic form of teaching when approaching ICT skills. There is a need for a structured curriculum for ICT skills and for ways of determining progression. Learners need to be supported in their exploration of ICT.

Recommendations for policy

Whilst this study is limited in scope – being a detailed study of a small group of tutors – it is possible to interpret these results within the context of the other studies that we have carried out in order to derive some recommendations for policy. Our study concentrated on a small group of tutors who were working within a Pathfinder Consortium, who were keen on using ICT, were identified by the Consortium as making good use of ICT and had their colleges' support in using ICT in the classroom.

We found that most of these tutors were relatively new to the use of ICT and their practice demonstrated that they were still at the early stages of developing approaches to using ICT in their teaching. They needed support in order to develop these skills further. It is a reasonable hypothesis that if this is the case for this group of tutors then it is going to be even more of an issue for tutors more generally. Our work with a range of tutors in **learndirect** centres (Kambouri, Mellar et al 2003) has shown that there are difficulties in training ICT specialists to take on basic skills teaching and so it is probably more effective to give basic skills tutors training in ICT use and time to prepare their sessions using ICT rather than attempting to train ICT specialists to support basic skills. We therefore recommend:

- Development of effective tutor training in the use of ICT in basic skills provision and support (including funding) for tutors during this training.

Again, the tutors we observed were in relatively privileged positions compared to many of their colleagues using ICT in basic skills teaching and had strong institutional support, nevertheless we observed a number of restrictions on their use of ICT due to difficulties with the ICT infrastructure – particularly the computer network – and were aware that at times that the teaching of basic skills was sometimes at the end of the queue for provision. Earlier work (Mellar, Kambouri et al., 2001) has shown this to be a widespread issue. We therefore recommend:

- Further development of ICT infrastructure (particularly computer networks) and higher priority to be given to provision of ICT for basic skills teaching.

The tutors we were working with were enthusiastic about using ICT in their teaching and more knowledgeable about ICT than many of the tutors we have talked to in other studies. Nevertheless their teaching as we observed it showed that they were often unclear about what aspects of ICT were valuable to their learners, there was little attention given to progression in ICT skills and little assessment that learners had achieved ICT objectives (as distinct from the literacy, numeracy and ESOL objectives). The range of ways in which ICT was introduced into the classroom that we observed both in this study and in our other studies shows that there is little agreement amongst tutors about what should be taught in this area. We therefore recommend:

■ Further development of the ICT skills curriculum and assessment methods[17]. Further consideration and debate about the nature of an ICT skills curriculum.[18]

Recommendations for further research

■ Building on the findings of the present study, a series of hypotheses about designs for effective use of ICT in basic skills should be generated and tested through intervention studies. Some of the themes to be explored are:
  – Targeting the use of ICT at specific literacy and numeracy learning objectives.
  – Collaborative learning with ICT.
  – Multimedia authoring as an approach to teaching literacy.
  – Computer-based problem-solving approaches to teaching numeracy.
  – Integrating ICT tutorial-based approaches into wider teaching patterns.
  – Using the communications aspects of ICT to encourage links between cultures and communities.
  – Developing learners' autonomy in their use of ICT resources.
  (This recommendation forms the basis for the design of the next study that we are carrying out as part of the work of the NRDC).
■ Observational studies of learners are needed in order to examine how learners are actually using the resources. This will be of particular importance in examining the use learners make of the Internet and hence the benefit that may be derived from this. We need to examine the ways in which informal learning occurs in this context.
■ Examination of the learning of ICT skills. The present study has been concerned principally with the way in which ICT is used to help learners in the areas of literacy and numeracy. A closer examination of the learning of ICT skills themselves is required.
■ Study of the ICT demands of the workplace to seek appropriate ways to introduce ICT skills that link with the work environment and needs.
■ Study the training of tutors in using ICT in basic skills provision. In particular it will be useful to compare the provision of ICT training to basic skills tutors (which is what we have seen in this present project) with the provision of basic skills training for ICT tutors (as we have seen in studies carried out for Ufi).

These studies need to be carried out bearing in mind the very specific context of adult literacy and numeracy, that is, the very wide range of backgrounds of learners and teachers and the uneven development of their basic skills. We need to examine which approaches work best with different categories of learners, for different levels of skills and for which aspects of the curriculum.

---

17. This study was carried out before the development of the standards for ICT as a skill for life (see http://www.qca.org.uk/qualifications/types/2791.html - accessed 18 May 2004). These draft standards do now provide a basis to enable tutors to ensure progression in the development of ICT skills (something that was lacking at the time of this study).
18. Discussion of some of the issues related to developing an appropriate curriculum are discussed in Computer Science and Telecommunications Board (1999), Carvin (2000) and humanITy (2003).

References and further reading

Askew, M., Brown, M., Rhodes, V., et al. (1997). **Effective teachers of numeracy.** King's College London

Bliss, J., M. Monk, et al. (1983). **Qualitative data analysis for educational research: a guide to uses of systemic networks.** London, Croom Helm.

Carvin, A. (2000) "More than Just Access", **EDUCAUSE Review,** November/December 2000. Available at http://www.educause.edu/pub/er/erm00/articles006/erm0063.pdf (accessed 18 May 2004).

Clarke, A. Englebright, L. (2003). **ICT – the new basic skill.** Leicester: NIACE.

Computer Science and Telecommunications Board (1999). **Being Fluent with Information Technology.** Washington, D.C.: National Academic Press.

Ginsburg, L. (1998) Integrating Technology into Adult Learning. **Technology, basic skills, and adult education: getting ready and moving forward.** C.E. Hopey. Ohio: ERIC Clearinghouse on Adult, Career, and Vocational Education, Ohio State University.

Hopey, C.E. (1998). **Technology, basic skills, and adult education: getting ready and moving forward.** Ohio: ERIC Clearinghouse on Adult, Career, and Vocational Education, Ohio State University.

humanITy (2003) Briefing paper no 1 ICT development and basic skills strategy, **humanITy: inclusion in the information age.** Available at: http://www.humanity.org.uk/articles/pub_ictdevelopment.shtml (accessed 30 January 2004).

Kambouri, M, Mellar, H. et al (2003) **Research into the effectiveness of learndirect materials and support system for learners with skills for life needs.** Report submitted to Ufi June 2003. Sheffield: Ufi. Available at: http://www.ufi.com/press/papers/IoE%20SFl%20Effectiveness.pdf (accessed 18 May 2004)

Kambouri, M. Schott, G. et al (2003) **Evaluating learndirect games for learners with skills for life needs.** Report, submitted to Ufl September 2003. Sheffield: Ufi. Available at http://www.ufi.com/press/papers/UFIGamesfinalreport.pdf (accessed 18 May 2004)

Mellar, H., Kambouri, M., Wolf, A., et al. (2001). **Research into the effectiveness of learning through ICT for people with basic skills needs.** Report submitted to Ufi June 2001. Sheffield: Ufi. Summary available at: http://www.ufi.com/press/papers/literacyguide.pdf (accessed 18 May 2004).

Mellar, H. and Kambouri, M. (2004). Learning and teaching adult basic skills with digital technology: research from the UK. **ICT and education: World Yearbook 2004: Digital technologies, communities and education.** A. Brown and N. Davis (eds), London: Kogan Page.

National Research and Development Centre for Adult Literacy and Numeracy, Institute of Education and The Basic Skills Agency (2003) **Using laptops to develop basic skills: a handbook for practitioners.** London: NRDC. Available at: http://www.nrdc.org.uk/uploads/documents/doc_2838.pdf – accessed 18 May 2004.

National Technology Laboratory for Literacy and Adult Education – TECH21. Online at: http://www.tech21.org/ (accessed 18 May 2004).

Pratt, D.D. et al (1998**). Five Perspectives on Teaching in Adult and Higher Education. Malabar**, FL: Krieger.

Ufi (2001) **Using ICT to develop literacy and numeracy: a guide for learning centres working with adult learners**. Sheffield: Ufi. Available at http://www.ufi.com/press/papers/literacyandnumeracy.pdf (accessed 18 May 2004).

Appendix 1: **Case studies**

The following reports summarise the observations for six of the eleven classes observed under a set of headings derived from the research questions, and listed in full in the **Pro-forma for summaries of observational data** in Appendix 3. Where a heading does not appear, this indicates that there was no evidence in the observations to enable a description to be given. The percentages given in these case studies refer to the percentage of the total number of five-minute observation units (not just those in which ICT was used) in which the described behaviour was the predominant behaviour during that observation.

PT – ESOL & ICT – Level 1

Background

There were 20 learners enrolled on this course, and the usual attendance was about 15. The class lasted two hours. The total number of observation units was 75 and in 3 per cent of these ICT was not the predominant activity. There were significant networking problems in these sessions. The main use was of desktop machine (89 per cent) with some use of a data projector (8 per cent). The main software used was educational software (37 per cent), followed by accessing the Web (27 per cent), and then office software (25 per cent). For the majority of the time, learners worked on their own computers (75 per cent) and there was no small group work observed. The main purpose of ICT use was to input practice material (41 per cent), followed by accessing new data (31 per cent) and then developing ICT skills (16 per cent). The tutor spent a lot of time addressing the class (72 per cent), somewhat less in discussion with learners (19 per cent) and some time in observing the learner (5 per cent).

The tutor often had to demonstrate procedures on his own desktop machine. There was a large screen, but this was on a side wall, and required a laptop, which was not always provided by the technicians on time.

1. Learning goals
What were the tutor's learning objectives?
This was an ESOL (Level 1) and ICT class.

Session	ICT objectives	Language objectives
1	Use the Internet to access information.	Find information about the borough of Hackney from provided websites. Answer a series of questions. write something about the borough.
2	Highlight words. Dragging and dropping. Use the thesaurus to find the meaning of words.	Become familiar with environmental issues. Learn relevant vocabulary.
3	Use the thesaurus. Move text. Use interactive software.	Continue theme of the environment. Write conditional sentences. Learn when to use conditional sentences.

How was the use of ICT integrated with the learning objectives?
All three sessions included both ICT and language objectives and the teaching of ICT was closely integrated with the language learning objectives. In session 1, ICT skills were addressed first and then the literacy skills, and in sessions 2 and 3 the literacy skills were addressed first and then the ICT skills. In each case both sets of skills were necessary in order to carry out the task.

To what extent was ICT seen as a basic skill?
ICT was not viewed as a subject in itself but rather as a tool for finding information (session 1) and for improving learners' English language (sessions 2 and 3), such as learning vocabulary and writing conditional sentences.

What were the forms of assessment used?
Informal assessment on an individual basis as the tutor visited learners and discussed their work with them. Learners were encouraged to print out their work as they went along in order to build up an ESOL portfolio.

2. Teaching

What happened in the sessions?

Session 1 (10/12/12)
Learners came in slowly at the start of the session, logged on to the network and the tutor gave out worksheets.

The tutor asked all the learners to come and look at his screen (there were 15 learners and it was hard for all of them to have a good view of the screen). He showed a range of different programs (e.g. Word, Netscape) and asked the learners to name them. He talked about how to hold the mouse and demonstrated how to open Netscape by double clicking. He then demonstrated the college intranet, how to access the library and search for information about the college. The tutor discussed search engines, introduced Google and described what was meant by hyperlinks.

The tutor went through the questions on the worksheet, asking the learners to say where they could search for answers. He pointed them to the website addresses that he had given on the worksheet. He then demonstrated how to search using a search engine, emphasising the need to limit the search and to read the results carefully.

Learners started going back to their computers, however a few stayed, and looked at his screen. The tutor asked if they were sure of what to do. More learners stopped and returned back to him. The tutor briefly ran through the demonstration again and then the learners returned to their seats.

The tutor circulated and helped learners as they worked on the tasks in the worksheet. Learners experienced problems due to the slow system, due to the fact that they had forgotten their password and also because they were unsure of what they had to do. Because of these problems the tutor spent a considerable amount of time with each learner visited.

The tutor asked learners to stop working and come and watch the large screen at the side of the room (as the technician had now brought the laptop). The learners were not accessing the sites that he had given them. The tutor showed the worksheet as a Word document and pointed out the websites in the text, showing the links indicated in blue. He asked the learners to find this document on the common drive and to access the websites via this document's links and demonstrated how to do this.

Some of the learners succeeded in retrieving the document from the common drive, but most continued working on what they were doing before. The tutor went around helping individual learners and asking them to retrieve the Word document. At the end he asked learners to save the Word file in their area and to log-off.

The initial aim of improving the use of the Internet for searching was largely not achieved. Learners who were already competent were able to use search engines, whereas learners who were not competent had to rely on the given links.

Session 2 (07/01/03)

Learners came in and logged-on. There were only eight learners present in this session and so it was easier for them to watch the tutor's screen. The tutor gave a PowerPoint presentation on what was to be the theme for next four sessions 'What is our environment?' The tutor worked through the presentation, explaining new words and concepts and questioning the learners. The tutor said that he would give them a floppy disk with various files on it. Using the data projector he demonstrated how to access the A: drive, how to access and open the text file, and how to use the down key and to scroll down the text using the mouse.

The tutor asked them to read the text and find words to do with the environment and said that if they found a word that they did not understand then they should use the thesaurus in Word and he demonstrated how this could be done.

The tutor went on to demonstrate how to find the highlighter from the tool bar, how to select the colour they wanted and asked them to highlight text that they did not understand. He explained that if they did not know what a toolbar symbol meant that leaving the cursor on the symbol would cause a message to appear. He reiterated how to access the A: drive and which way to insert the disk.

Learners worked on their computers and the tutor circulated and helped them with individual problems, such as inserting the disk, finding the appropriate file, saving files, highlighting words and using the thesaurus.

The tutor asked the class to go back to view the projected screen, and he showed them an exercise in which definitions were matched alongside words, sometimes incorrectly. He showed how they could highlight a definition and then drag it to the appropriate word. The tutor said that they had to be careful as sometimes it could go wrong and he illustrated that if it did go wrong, that they could use the undo button. He went on to highlight some text and use the cut button explaining that the text has not gone forever, only temporarily. Learners looked puzzled and the tutor demonstrated how to paste the text back into the document.

Learners returned to work and the tutor circulated discussing the meaning of terms generated by the thesaurus and whether they were relevant. One learner had finished and had typed the new related words in a different colour. The tutor called the class to come and see it and asked her to explain how she had done it; they dispersed and tried to do the same.

The tutor reiterated instructions for saving and asked the learners to save their work. He then set the homework and the learners logged-off.

Session 3 (14/01/03)

Learners came in and logged-on. The tutor called the class together around a computer and he asked them how individuals could improve the environment. One learner referred to cycling and because the tutor knew that the learner's bicycle had been stolen he developed this into a series of examples of conditional sentences, which was followed by a brief discussion of forms of conditional sentences.

The tutor asked learners to watch an introductory presentation and to identify what type of software it was (PowerPoint). He also showed an animated cartoon of a cyclist interspersed with conditional sentences, and asked questions regarding the form of the conditional sentences.

The tutor demonstrated how to access the Tense Buster[19] program, directed them to the section on conditional sentences and asked them to work at the intermediate level. He explained that this program would give them feedback about the answers that they gave. The learners worked on their own and the tutor circulated checking their exercises and the sentences that they had created and made suggestions. The tutor reminded learners to save the work they had done in Word and to log off. The learners were not able to save the work that they had done with Tense Buster.

What was the tutor's style of teaching?

The tutor always introduced tasks by clearly describing them in a whole class presentation and then summarising the procedures at the end of the presentation. When task instructions were given, learners were usually either gathered around the tutor's desktop machine or the laptop connected to the data projector, which projected onto the side of the room. Because of this arrangement learners were not able to practice procedures whilst they were being demonstrated and were not able to take notes. The tutor did not provide handouts with the procedures written down. As the task instructions were often quite complex for those with limited ICT skills the learners found it difficult to remember what they were supposed to do and so needed a lot of individual support. The tutor circulated and helped individuals, but he needed to spend a significant time with each learner and so learners often had to rely on other learners for help.

How were the necessary ICT skills taught?

The ICT skills needed for the tasks set were taught through demonstration and through individual support. The tutor introduced many ICT skills and ICT terminology in a short time without perhaps giving learners sufficient opportunity to practice them and it was therefore essential to support learners individually.

How did the tutor manage the classroom?

The tutor addressed the whole class at the beginning of each new task and then asked them to work individually. Transitions to and from using computers were made by the tutor raising his voice to get attention, asking learners to come close to him and watch his computer screen or projected screen on the side wall. These transitions to and from using computers were not made very smoothly because learners had to leave their seats.

3. ICT

How was ICT used in the classroom?

ICT was used as the main tool for teaching the literacy objectives.

---

19 Published by Clarity - http://www.clarity.com.hk/index.htm - accessed 18 May 2004

Were there any situations where the use of ICT may have acted as a barrier to learning or teaching?

Here are two examples of learners for whom ICT acted as a barrier to learning during session 1

- H did not know what to do. The tutor did not get to her for some time. When he did get to her he helped her to access the first of the websites listed in the worksheet. As soon as the tutor left, H was stuck again and so she approached other learners and asked for their help. They demonstrated what she had to do, but still she was not sure of what to do. Towards the end of the session the tutor gave her a handout that would help her to answer at least the first three questions, H logged-off and left.
- A had forgotten her password and this delayed her starting the lesson. She did not know what to do and needed support. She constantly asked the learner next to her for directions and they also talked in their mother tongue.

Were there any technological failures?

The tutor did not invite us to the college earlier in the year because of technical problems with the college computer system.

In the first session observed the system was very slow. It took learners a great deal of time to log on and to access the Internet or open a Word document (one learner was not able to start working until 50 minutes after the session began). Learners were frustrated and unsure of what they should do because they did not know whether it was the system's fault or whether they had done something wrong themselves.

The tutor had requested a laptop for the introduction of the session. The technician did not deliver it on time – he was almost an hour late – and thus the tutor could not use it as planned. The lesson plan read: 'Set scene. SS have just moved to borough; they have a family with 2 small children and want to find out more about what it has to offer. What sort of things would they want to know?'. The tutor was unable to set out this imaginary scene for the learners and so they were unsure why they were searching for specific information. When the tutor tried to use the laptop, he found that it was not connected to the Internet and therefore he could not demonstrate how to access websites through a Word document with active links. So he displayed the document, pointed to the active links and told the learners that if they clicked on these, they would be taken to these sites, but was unable to demonstrate this.

4. Learning

How did the learners work with each other?

The computer room was arranged for individual working and learners were expected to work individually to achieve the set tasks. However, they were free to co-operate and frequent interactions among learners were observed. There was less interaction in session 2 because there were fewer learners and the tutor was able to deal with queries more quickly.

Did the literacy level of learners impact upon their use of ICT?

There were big differences in literacy skills of the learners and the tutor discouraged those with better literacy skills helping the others, as they tended to do the work for them.

GS2 – ESOL – Foundation and English for Young Adults – entry 2/3

Background

There were 18 learners enrolled on this course, and the usual attendance was about 16. The class lasted one and a half hours. Total number of observation units was 60 and in 8 per cent of these ICT was not the predominant activity. There were no ICT technical problems. The main use was of desktop machines (72 per cent), with some use of a data projector (10 per cent) and of simultaneous projector and desktop use (10 per cent). The main software used was office software (52 per cent), with accessing the Web (17 per cent), communication (10 per cent) next and a small use of educational software (5 per cent). For the majority of the time learners worked on their own (60 per cent), though there was some paired working (10 per cent). The main purpose of ICT use was for inputting practice material (35 per cent), a significant amount of time was devoted to entering data (27 per cent) and accessing data (18 per cent). A small amount of time was devoted primarily to developing ICT skills (7 per cent). The tutor spent a lot of time addressing the class (53 per cent), somewhat less time in discussion with the learners (28 per cent) and some time in observation of the class (15 per cent).

The classroom was small and contained 23 computers. Physical space constrained what could be done with the class and made it difficult to walk around in the class.

1. Learning goals

What were the tutor's learning objectives?

The class was described as FEYA (Foundation and English for Young Adults 16–21) plus ICT and was directed at learners at entry 2/3 Level. The primary aim was to improve communications, and accuracy in writing, and this was done by using WebCT (email, bulletin board, and chat) for communication between two groups of learners. The other group had originally been a Brazilian group but at the time of the observation was South Thames College.

Session	ICT objectives	Language objectives
1	Select items from drop down menu. Send, receive and reply to email messages. Enter text in form fields. Follow hyperlinks.	Improve awareness of structure and purpose of a text. Identify sections of an email message. Write and reply to invitations (accepting and refusing).
2	Send, receive and reply to email messages. Enter text in form fields. Follow hyperlinks.	Improve awareness of the importance of accuracy in writing. Discuss ways to formulate sentences and layout an email message. Practice correcting mistakes.
3	Access information on the Internet. Check email and follow instructions. Download a file. Fill in a Word interactive worksheet, save it and print. Reply to email.	Discuss learners' country profiles. Predict information about learners' countries.

Session	ICT objectives	Language objectives
4	Check email. Follow hyperlinks. Find information on a given website. Create text in Word. Check work for errors and save. Post contributions to discussion area on WebCT.	Convert notes into sentences. Write a paragraph about learner's country.

How did these match to the learners' goals?
In general, all learners seemed to be well motivated and involved, enjoyed the lessons and were able to achieve the lesson objectives.

How was the use of ICT integrated with the learning objectives?
The development of ICT skills was closely integrated with the language learning objectives within the lesson plans. Learners used computers throughout the sessions. The reading, writing and record-keeping parts of the sessions were all carried out on-screen. Speaking and listening activities took place either in the whole group or in small groups. The tutor fully integrated the data projector into his teaching, using it to present tasks, give examples and review activities.

The teaching of ICT skills and language skills were well integrated, with ICT being used as the main tool for achieving the language objectives. Learners would not be able to achieve the language objectives unless they mastered the required ICT skills, such as being able to communicate through emails, open attachments, attach documents, follow hyperlinks, etc.

To what extent was ICT seen as a basic skill?
ICT was not viewed as a subject in itself but rather as a tool and specifically as a communication tool. During all four sessions learners were familiarising themselves with WebCT and email. Progression in ICT skills was informally assessed by the tutor's observation of the learners' achievement of the lesson objectives.

What were the forms of assessment used?
At the end of each session the tutor led a discussion in which the learners told each other what they had learnt and wrote it in their record of work. However, due to limited time, the tutor usually took control of the discussion and directed learners in what to say and what to write. The tutor always checked learners' work and when learners completed their tasks before the end of the session, they emailed their work to him. They were also asked to email him their homework.

2. Teaching
What happened in the sessions?
Session 1 (19/11/02)
The tutor explained the shape of the lesson and asked learners to check their email and download a document. The exercise involved reading an email invitation and answering questions about the email by either selecting an answer from a list or by typing in the answer. The tutor moved round the room questioning learners when they were stuck and commenting on their answers. At one point the tutor advised learners to use an online dictionary to check the meaning of words. When most of the learners had finished, the tutor asked the learners

to stop working and tell him the answers to the questions. These were displayed on the projected screen and learners completed or corrected their exercise.

The tutor asked the learners to form groups of three to discuss responses to the email. He assigned a different 'role' for each learner. After a few minutes the tutor asked learners for their responses. Then the tutor asked them to send an email replying to the invitation. The tutor circulated commenting on their writing, explaining grammar points and making suggestions for improvements. Learners were asked to copy their email into a Word document, check the spelling and grammar, replace their response with the corrected one, and then send their email.

The tutor asked the learners what they had learnt that day, rephrased their responses and typed them up. Learners copied from the projector to their 'record sheet' on the computer. Finally, the tutor explained the homework.

Session 2 (3/12/02)

The tutor discussed what they would be doing in the lesson, demonstrated on the projector work done by the class to date, thanked them and encouraged them to continue. The tutor asked learners to email him their homework and demonstrated how to do this.

The tutor discussed the previous week's lesson in which they had communicated with another college and demonstrated the chat facility. Learners had problems accessing chat, so the tutor asked them to switch their monitors off and he demonstrated again. The learners then accessed and used chat. They then accessed a Word document with language errors for them to work on via their WebCT email.

In order to get the learners' attention, he again asked them to turn their monitors off and he projected a message from the previous week and discussed how it could be improved, and edited the most serious mistakes with the whole class. The tutor assigned learners to small groups and told them to have only one monitor switched on per group. He then sent emails with documents for learners to work on. Learners started working and the tutor walked around the class dealing with individual problems.

The tutor instructed the class to stop working and to fill in their 'record of work'. He questioned learners and typed up the record of work, projected on the large screen for them to copy.

Session 3 (21/01/03)

The tutor instructed learners to access the Internet and complete a college survey. He then introduced the aims of the lesson and asked the learners to check their email account and work according to the instructions they found there.

The tutor observed the learners working without giving them any help for about ten minutes, and then began to circulate and help individuals. He kept the interventions to a minimum and instead encouraged learners to read instructions carefully and to help each other when they had a problem.

The tutor checked his email account to see how many learners had sent him their work and then sent them a new email with further instructions. He walked around, reminded learners to read instructions carefully and helped with individual problems. The tutor checked his email account and praised learners for the work they had done.

The tutor instructed learners to discuss with a partner what they had done. He then asked them to complete their record of work, which they did together with the tutor putting up the record on the projector and the learners copying.

Session 4 (28/01/03)

The tutor asked learners to turn their monitors off and through a question and answer session he revised last week's lesson. The tutor then introduced the aims of the lesson, one of which was for the learners to work as much as possible on their own and if they had problems to discuss them with each other. The tutor gave general instructions and asked a learner to repeat them. He then instructed learners to access their email in order to receive more detailed instructions.

Learners worked for more than an hour on the tasks given. For the first 20 minutes the tutor simply observed. As each learner's work was completed, the tutor went through it checking, questioning and making suggestions. Occasionally, if there was a point the tutor considered of interest to the whole class, he attracted their attention and explained it via the projected computer screen.

The tutor demonstrated where they were to save their work, but this was quite complex and the tutor went around the class making sure that each person did it correctly.

By the end of this session the learners were able to read mail, send mail to more than one recipient, attach files and download files. They were able to edit documents and insert pictures.

What was the tutor's style of teaching?

The tutor adopted an apprenticeship perspective on teaching, presenting a carefully ordered set of tasks leading from simple to complex and encouraging the development of greater learner autonomy.

At the beginning of each lesson the tutor provided learners with the learning objectives of the lesson and demonstrated to learners what he wanted them to do. Whilst the learners were working he provided support, questioning them, correcting errors in their writing, making suggestions for improvement, directing them to appropriate resources, helping with ICT problems and emphasising the need to pay attention to the instructions given. At the end of each session, the tutor summarised what had been learnt.

The tutor tried to anticipate what learners could do on their own and where they needed help. He set out to develop the learners' autonomy, and therefore as learners became more competent in their ICT skills, his role changed; he offered fewer directions and gave more responsibility to learners to complete tasks on their own. He encouraged learners to support each other and offer appropriate help. In the later sessions as they became more independent learners he spent more time observing without intervening.

How were the necessary ICT skills taught?

ICT skills were mainly taught through demonstration to the whole class and then with individual support to those who were still unsure of how to do it. In demonstrating how to use the chat facilities the tutor found that most learners had not understood his initial demonstration and so he asked them to switch off their monitors and he demonstrated the procedures again.

The tutor sometimes taught specific ICT skills to individuals or small groups, talking them through the procedure step by step but not taking control of their computer. When learners were having difficulty with something that had been covered in a previous session, the tutor asked other learners to help them.

How did the tutor manage the classroom?
The tutor addressed the whole class at the beginning of each new task and then asked them to work individually or in small groups. Transitions to and from using the computers were made smoothly by the tutor raising his voice to get attention, sometimes asking learners to turn off their screens, putting a screen image on the projector and drawing the learners' attention to it.

The tutor said that he would have liked to have control over the learners' monitors so that he could blank them out when he wanted to get everyone's attention.

3. ICT
How was ICT used in the classroom?
ICT was the main tool for teaching and it was used throughout all sessions. The teaching materials were often delivered to learners via email and learners also sent in their work via email.

4. Learning
How did the learners work with each other?
For most of the class the learners used computers either individually or, when asked, worked in small groups. Learners were free to interact with each other when they had problems.

The tutor aimed at promoting autonomy and less dependency on him. So, he encouraged learners to interact with each other frequently and ask for help whenever they did not understand. In session 4, the tutor told the learners that one of the session's aims was for them to work on their own as much as possible. If learners had problems they should read the instructions again, if they still had a problem, they should ask their classmates and if they still had a problem then they could ask him. He emphasised the need to give clear explanations and he intervened when he observed learners doing the work for other learners instead of explaining to them how to do it.

Did the learners' levels of ICT skills impact upon their learning?
In this class, learners had to be able to use ICT in order to be able to achieve the literacy aims of the class. However, there was no evidence that constituted a problem for anyone in the class.

CN – literacy – level 2

Background

There were 14 learners enrolled on this course, and the usual attendance was about ten. The class lasted two hours. Total number of observations in sessions 1–3 (session 4 was devoted to learner observation) was 72. In 29 per cent ICT was not the predominant activity. There were no ICT technical problems. All actual use of ICT was of desktop machines. The main use was of office software (42per cent), with some use of educational software (18 per cent) and some use of the Web for accessing information (4 per cent). Learners usually worked on their own when using ICT (50 per cent) but there was a significant element of small group work (21 per cent). The major purpose for ICT use was for practice (58 per cent), with some use for accessing data (7 per cent) and developing ICT skills (6 per cent). The tutor spent relatively little time addressing the class (21 per cent) and spent most of her time in discussion with learners (63 per cent).

1. Learning goals

What were the tutor's learning objectives?

This was a Literacy course – Level 2. The learners had two sessions with this tutor during the days that sessions were observed. Computers were used only during the afternoon sessions. The morning sessions were used for teaching and the afternoon ICT-based sessions for practice.

Session	Objectives
1	Join words – using colour and mouse movement to reinforce memory. Use the Internet to research immigration patterns into East London.
2	Join words in sentences – using colour and mouse movement to reinforce memory. Use a word processor to change writing (and so learners can change their minds about language decisions without the effort of re-writing).
3	Word process second drafts of assignments. Use BBC Skillswise website to consolidate work on joining sentences.
4	Become familiar with research using the Internet. Compare on-line and paper-based research methods.

How did these match to the learners' goals?

The great majority of the learners enjoyed using computers for learning, the one learner who did not like using computers was given the alternative of finding information needed from the library and so the tutor was able to accommodate all learners' needs.

How was the use of ICT integrated with the learning objectives?

The literacy objectives were the primary objectives and ICT was used as a tool for practicing literacy skills.

To what extent was ICT seen as a basic skill?

ICT was not seen as a subject in itself by the tutor. In interview the tutor said: 'I am not an IT person, sometimes the students know more about computers than me'.

What were the forms of assessment used?

The tutor only provided assessment of their literacy skills. As she moved around the class she discussed their work with learners making suggestions for improvement, checking answers, occasionally marking work and always collecting their work to correct later.

2. Teaching

What happened in the sessions?

Class was in the afternoon of a whole-day session in which learners used the computers to develop and practice language concepts that had been worked on in the morning session. The classroom was large and learners had plenty of space for writing and using the computers. Small numbers of learners: nine in session 1, six in session 2, ten in session 3, and eight in session 4.

Session 1 (28/11/02)

The tutor recapped the morning session, introduced the aims of the afternoon session and gave out a worksheet. The tutor explained how to work on the computers and suggested that learners inexperienced with computers could pair up with more experienced learners. Six learners decided to work in pairs and three individually.

The tutor wrote on a board the path to follow to find teaching materials that they were to use. She then circulated making sure that learners could drag words and that they understood punctuation.

As learners finished the first task, the tutor gave to each one a second worksheet, writing on the board the URL of the website that they were to use. Then, the tutor circulated and helped with punctuation and ICT problems.

When most learners had finished, the tutor addressed the whole class and introduced the second part of the lesson; finding information from the Internet. The learners were doing research for a project on immigration patterns in Tower Hamlets. She wrote up the URLs for some search engines. She then circulated in class and talked to learners about how they could get the information they needed for the work they were writing.

The tutor stopped learners working and asked for their impressions about working with computers. She then assigned homework.

Session 2 (05/12/02)

The tutor gave each learner two worksheets and read them through explaining what learners had to do. She wrote on the board the path to follow for the one task. Learners were free to choose the task they wanted to do first. The tutor circulated and checked that all learners were on task. The tutor spent the rest of the time interacting individually with learners. She went around and spent time with each learner discussing their work, making suggestions for improvement and helping with literacy and ICT problems.

Session 3 (12/12/02)

Learners worked individually, some at computers and some at desks. The tutor was not in class because the morning session had overrun. When she came in, she walked around and observed briefly what they were doing.

The tutor gave out handouts about Level 2 accreditation. She addressed the whole class and explained the first three points. She answered learners' questions and asked learners to complete materials for submission for accreditation. The tutor collected drafts and praised learners.

The tutor introduced the BBC Skillswise as a website for revision and practice and wrote the URL for the site on the board. She then circulated interacting individually with learners, who were working on a range of different tasks, discussing their work, helping with problems, making suggestions, collecting work, checking and marking it and praising learners.

Session 4 (23/1/03)

This session was part of an ongoing project on research about immigration in Tower Hamlets. The learners had discussed the backgrounds of immigrant groups in Tower Hamlets and they were each assigned the task of finding information about a specific immigrant population.

At the start of the session the tutor reminded learners about the group they needed to find information for, e.g. Jewish, Bangladeshi, etc. and ran over the kind of information they needed to find e.g. (a) why did they come? (b) size of population now (c) type of business and (d) country. She then gave a short introduction to search engines, including giving a brief description of what the Google initial page looks like and what the page of the results might look like. She also talked about appropriate search terms and encouraged learners to use more than one site.

The following descriptions outline the activities of a number of learners, each of whom was observed for 20 minutes:

Learner A logged on quickly, accessed the internet, went to Google, and entered 'Chinese in London'. He was not happy with the results and so tried different search terms: 'Chinese in Tower Hamlets'. He clicked on the first result, but the page could not be displayed, so he went back to the results page and clicked on similar pages and found what he saw as a 'useful' site. He quickly identified the section that interested him (on Chinese immigrants), he copied it, opened a Word document and pasted it. He then returned to the web page and read further. At this point the tutor came by and watched what he was doing. She commented that he would not get all the information needed from one page and that he will probably need to look for another web page. She watched him for a while. A copied another part of the text and pasted it into his Word document. A appeared to have good ICT skills. He easily selected the parts of the text that he wants, right-clicked to select copy and pasted them into his Word document. He changed the fonts and numbered the points that he pasted in.

Learner B had already visited 2–3 sites and printed out some pages. He said that this was the first time that they had used search engines in this class but that he knew how to search because he has done this frequently at home. He likes using computers in classes, and takes another class in which language and ICT work are combined. He was confident and had good ICT skills and needed little support from the tutor. The initial instructions given by the tutor were enough. He read an article, printed out just those pages that provided the information he was looking for. After printing something he quickly went through the printout, marking relevant parts and underlining words.

Learner C was looking at a number of web pages, going through them and printing some of them out. He appeared to be confident in his use of ICT and said that he enjoyed using computers. He was looking for information on Black Africans and managed to find a few pieces of information but he was not very pleased with the quality of the information. He said that the tutor told him to go to the library (because 'books are of a better quality'). He intended to go to the library and hoped to find more detailed and useful information there.

Learner D had been in the library, she sat down at the computer. She said that she had not found the library book that she found very useful for her because it discussed Black-African immigrants in the UK generally and did not provide any specific information about Tower Hamlets. She preferred the information she found on the internet, she was very pleased with the results. She had accessed a number of sites and was able to rapidly identify material she felt was worth more careful reading. She said that she had used search-engines before but that she had not been very confident and that she had learnt more in this class.

At the end of the session the tutor stopped the learners and re-stated the aims of the lesson: to produce a group report, with each learner writing one section of it. They briefly discussed what the report should be like: factual, using formal language, with a structured layout and incorporating tables and charts.

What was the tutor's style of teaching?
The tutor gave the task instructions at the beginning of each session and then got learners to start working. She then visited each individual and made sure that they were working on task. Learners were free to choose how to work (paper work or computer work, pairs or individuals), they were free to choose what task to do first and they were free to interact frequently with each other and help/support each other.

How were the necessary ICT skills taught?
At the beginning of each lesson, the tutor explained to learners what they were to do and how they should use the computers, sometimes writing notes, URLs, etc. on the board, but there were no demonstrations of ICT procedures. ICT skills were mostly taught as the tutor helped learners when they had ICT problems (such as use of cursors, accessing Word, and different ways to 'rub out').

How did the tutor manage the classroom?
At the start of the session, the tutor explained clearly what the aim of the afternoon was and the tasks that they were expected to complete. There was little formal teaching in these afternoon sessions, which were a follow-up to the more formal morning sessions.

At the start of the session learners sat at desks in the centre of the classroom and then moved to computers, which were placed around the classroom. The transition between whole class discussion and ICT use was done smoothly. As the learners were working on computers, the tutor went round the class, checking work, making suggestions and solving any language or ICT problems.

3. ICT
How was ICT used in the classroom?
ICT was used as a means for practicing literacy skills.

4. Learning
How did the learners work with each other?
In the main, learners worked individually because they had to produce work for accreditation, but they were left free to interact with others or work in pairs, if they preferred to co-operate.

In session 1, the tutor suggested that less ICT skilled learners should be paired with more skilled learners. Six learners chose to work in pairs and three chose to work individually. There was lots of discussion not only within pairs, but also across the whole class. Paired work on the computers was mainly due to the lack of computers for individual work and when the adjacent classroom became available, most learners chose to work individually.

Was ICT used in such a way as to enable a match to learners' learning styles or preferences?
The main indication of a matching to learning styles was in the area of ICT itself. The tutor gave learners the option of using ICT or to use paper and if learners did not want to use computers then they could write their work by hand.

Did the literacy level of learners impact upon their use of ICT?
Learners had a high level of literacy (Level 2) and that impacted positively for example upon their use of search engines in session 4. Learners came across lots of information and they were able to quickly decide whether the information presented was useful or not.

Did the learners' levels of ICT skills impact upon their learning?
In general learners were able to achieve the tasks set by the tutor and learners did not appear to be frequently stuck because of their ICT skills. Some learners had better ICT skills than others, and learners would ask support from their classmates or their tutor. However, there was one learner with low ICT skills who was frequently stuck and needed support with both her literacy skills and ICT skills. The support was provided by the tutor and by classmates who were sitting close to her.

SG – literacy with PCs – entry 3/Level 1

Background
There were 12 learners enrolled on this course, and the usual attendance was about eight. The class lasted two hours. The total number of observation units was 81, in 15 per cent ICT was not the predominant activity. There were very few ICT technical problems (2 per cent). The most commonly observed style of use was for the learners to be working with desktop machines (68 per cent), and there was some use of a data projector (5 per cent). The main use of ICT was of office software (68 per cent) and some use of educational software (10 per cent). Learners usually worked on their own with computers (64 per cent) and there was no small group work. The main purpose of ICT use was for practice (54 per cent), with some entering of data (19 per cent) and development of ICT skills (6 per cent). The tutor spent most of the time in discussion with learners (53 per cent), with a significant amount of time was spent in talking to the class as a whole (40 per cent).

1. Learning goals

What were the tutor's learning objectives?
The tutor had both ICT and literacy aims, he was concerned to improve the learners' use of punctuation and their skills in using Word.

Session	ICT objectives	Literacy objectives
1	Modify paragraphs and margins. Use bullets points.	Write notes using '!' and '?'
2		Complete writing assignments with punctuation.
3	Practice ICT skills. Use spellcheck.	Reinforce punctuation. Punctuate 7/10 sentences correctly. Punctuate lists correctly. Punctuate 80% Nazreddin story. Write a letter using punctuation correctly (., Capitals letters, !, and ?)
4	Draw shapes using Drawing toolbar.	Reinforce punctuation. Do some comprehension. Get 70% of Nazreddin Quiz correct. Get 70% in punctuation exercises.

How did these match to the learners' goals?
The tutor had changed the name of this class from 'ICT and Literacy' to 'Literacy with a PC' to indicate that the emphasis would be on literacy rather than ICT, though computers would be frequently used.

The tutor used a short questionnaire to ascertain learners' views about using computers in their learning. It appeared that most learners chose this class because they wanted to improve both their literacy and ICT skills and they enjoyed using computers. Only one of them wrote that she did not really mind if they were using computers or not and one other was not confident in computer use. The learners wanted to learn more about how to use Word and the tutor tried to accommodate their needs. In the second and third session one learner made significant use of drawing facilities and other learners wanted to do this as well, and so, in the fourth session the tutor set out to teach the use of the drawing toolbar.

How was the use of ICT integrated with the learning objectives?
For most of the time the literacy objectives were seen as primary and the ICT supported those aims. However, there was a clear intention to develop ICT skills as well and learners also welcomed this aspect. In session 4, the use of drawing within Word was an ICT skills dominated activity and was seen as motivational rather than directly connected to the literacy aims of the class.

To what extent was ICT seen as a basic skill?
Literacy and ICT skills were both seen as important, though literacy skills took precedence. ICT was also seen as a useful teaching tool.

What were the forms of assessment used?
The tutor provided feedback to learners as he circulated, and he collected completed

assignments at the end of the session, which he returned at the following session. ICT skills were assessed informally as the tutor helped learners with problems relating to the use of ICT tools.

2. Teaching

What happened in the sessions?

Session 1 (25/11/02)

The tutor began the lesson with a warm-up game using the data projector to show different coloured cards with letters on them and talked about favourite colours. He then recapped on the previous week's work and introduced the topics for this lesson: the use of bullet points for lists and the writing of informal letters.

Using the data projector the tutor built up a list of ingredients for a recipe and then demonstrated how to add bullets and how to customise fonts and bullets by changing size and colour and also demonstrated how to create their own bullets.

The learners followed his demonstration and then tried for themselves, whilst the tutor walked around the class dealing with individual problems. The learners then accessed a worksheet on the network that asked them to write a shopping list with ten items and then to write instructions for changing a baby's nappy. The first list was to have bullet points and the second was to be numbered. There was some discussion about what sort of things to write on the shopping list and learners began the activity working individually at computers. The tutor walked around the class dealing with individual problems. When learners completed the assignments, the tutor asked the learners to swap printouts, and to read each other's work and comment – suggesting improvements and changes.

The tutor next asked the learners to write a letter to a friend and to demonstrate their understanding of how to use punctuation in the letter. He asked them to plan their letters first, either on screen or on paper. The learners worked individually on the task and the tutor assisted by moving around the class, making suggestions and answering questions about their writing. The tutor used the white board to record elicited suggestions for ending informal letters and discussed with the learners how they ended letters in their own languages.

The tutor finished the session by recapping on the lesson by asking learners what they had done and what they had learnt.

Session 2 (2/12/02)

The tutor began the lesson with a warm-up game and then briefly revised the points that the learners should have in mind in order to write good sentences. The tutor talked about the assignments that they had been working on (speeches, notes, letters and list) and he gave them back their work asking them to correct them. The learners worked individually and mainly independently, retrieved their documents from the network and corrected them. The tutor walked around the class dealing with individual problems (both literacy and ICT problems).

Session 3: (9/12/02)

The tutor began the lesson with a warm-up game and then introduced the main topic of the lesson, which was to work on spelling, punctuation and then on writing letters. The tutor discussed punctuation, wrote up a complex sentence on the white board and then added the punctuation in discussion with the class. This was repeated several times for several other sentences. The tutor then demonstrated how learners could access a Word document with the punctuation exercises that he had prepared and he then walked around the class dealing with individual problems.

When the learners had completed the assignment, the tutor used the data projector to demonstrate how to use spellcheck. He then dictated three sentences, including punctuation. Some learners entered these directly into Word, others wrote them on paper and then typed them up later. The tutor asked them to use spellcheck to make sure that they had spelt the words correctly.

The tutor then set up a competition between two teams, asking them to write down as many words as they could think of that rhymed with the words he gave.

The tutor asked the learners to write a letter. He first demonstrated how to find a Word document with the instructions that he had prepared and then asked them to work individually. He walked around the class dealing with individual problems (both literacy and ICT problems).

The tutor recapped on the lesson by asking learners what they had done and what they had learnt.

Session 4 (16/12/02)

In the first part of the session the learners worked on punctuation exercises with a teaching program – 'Issues in English'.

Learner S was observed closely whilst working on this program. She followed the tutor's instructions, found the worksheet, printed it out and followed the instructions on it. She was eager to start working and she asked the tutor twice about the level that she should use. The tutor told her to wait for a while and then he demonstrated how to use the program. During the demonstration the tutor asked questions and S participated. The tutor asked two learners to work on Level 3 and the others on Level 2. With the software the learners could read a text and at the same time listen to someone speaking the text, some words were highlighted in red and learners could read an explanation of the word if they clicked on the word. S listened to the story, read the definition of some words and while waiting for the tutor to tell the class what to do next, she started 'playing' with the programme; clicking buttons and seeing what happened. The tutor asked them to access a punctuation exercise.

S started but became frustrated because she could not 'undo' a command and because she only got two sentences out of ten correct. The program gave no other feedback. When S did the exercise again, she noticed that at the bottom of the page, the number of correct sentences were noted and so she could determine whether the last answer was correct or not. S repeated the exercises, but this time asked for the tutor's help because she wanted to get more than two correct. The tutor avoided helping her saying that he would not always be around to help them and that she needed to do it by herself. S again got only two correct sentences. Now, she asked more insistently for the tutor's help. The tutor went to her and watched her inserting the punctuation marks. He reminded her not to forget to put full stops and S then got eight sentences correct. She still wanted to get ten out of ten and so she repeated the exercise. This time she got only seven out of ten. She was not satisfied and so she repeated the exercise again. With the tutor's help, she now got nine out of ten. S was frustrated because she did not manage to get ten out of ten. At the beginning she was excited but after repeating the exercise many times without getting them all correct, she was anxious. She wanted to get full marks.

The tutor pointed her to a practice exercise for the exercise she was trying to do. In the practice exercise the program indicated how many punctuation marks were required for each sentence and it would not allow the insertion of a wrong punctuation mark. S was excited and got all 13 sentences correct. She informed her tutor and he told her to repeat the main exercise. S was very eager to do this. The first time she got eight sentences correct, the second time she got nine sentences correct and finally the third time she got everything correct. She was really pleased and said out loud that she got everything correct. She then printed the results and showed them to her tutor.

In the second part of the lesson the tutor directed the learners to a Word document with instructions for drawing shapes in Word. The tutor demonstrated the Draw toolbar. Most learners repeated what the tutor was doing but one learner could not keep up with the tutor's instructions. This learner had good literacy skills but struggled with the ICT skills. The drawing work was particularly difficult for her because she could not derive any support from her literacy skills. Too much information was presented in too short a time for her and she was completely lost. She could not handle the mouse very skillfully and much of the time she could not click where she wanted to. The provided worksheet did not give instructions as to what the learners were to do, but rather introduced some of the drawing functions and suggested that the learners explore. This learner did not enjoy the exercise.

What was the tutor's style of teaching?
The tutor talked to the class about the work for the session, offered examples on the board and then showed them where they could find the assignments on the network. The learners were working mainly on their own and the tutor would check with them that they had understood the instructions. The tutor exercised strong control over what the learners were doing. Learners were free to ask for help (from the tutor or other learners), but they were expected to work on task and to produce individual work.

How were the necessary ICT skills taught?
The majority of the learners in this class already had the necessary ICT skills to open and work on Word documents. However, the tutor aimed at improving their ICT skills, such as adding and customising bullet points, customising a paragraph, using spellcheck and using the Draw toolbar. He demonstrated the procedures using the data projector and then talked with learners individually to make sure that they knew what to do.

How did the tutor manage the classroom?
The tutor wanted to start the session by introducing the lesson aims to the whole class. However, when learners came in they tended to log in to the network, so he used an icebreaker activity in order to gain their attention and to draw them away from the computers. He said that he would prefer it if the learners were not constantly in front of computers, and that it would be ideal to have two different spaces: a space with a round table and a space for the computers.

3. ICT

How was ICT used in the classroom?
ICT was widely used in these sessions, principally as a means of teaching. The tutor used the

college intranet to distribute the assignments and learners did all their assignments. In one session interactive educational software was used to support the teaching of punctuation. In this same session learners were also encouraged to explore the drawing capabilities of Word, just as a (rather playful) activity in its own right.

Were there any situations where the use of ICT may have acted as a barrier to learning or teaching?
There was one learner for whom ICT may have acted as a barrier to learning. In using 'Issues in English' she found it difficult to progress because she could not handle the mouse very well and indeed she appeared to be afraid to use it. However, she had chosen to do this class – which was an optional class for her. She was aware of her lack of confidence in using computers and she may well have chosen this class as a way of improving her ICT skills.

There was an interactive white board in this classroom, the only one in Tower Hamlets College. The tutor noted that he did not know how to use it. There was a special pen that did not work; the tutor thought that the battery in it was flat. The tutor was using the interactive white board as a large projector screen.

Were there any technological failures?
There was only one incident of technological failure, when a website was not available. The tutor had come into class before the learners arrived and checked the site and so he was able to modify his plans and the lesson was not disrupted. The website became accessible later and so the tutor was able to incorporate this work later in the session.

4. Learning
How did the learners work with each other?
Learners were encouraged to work individually because their assignments would be used for their accreditation. However, there was a very friendly classroom climate and learners frequently asked for the tutor's help. When the tutor was with a learner, other learners who needed help took the initiative to approach the person sitting next to them and asked for help. Learners were asked to work in pairs or trios only in one session, when they were asked to read each other's work and on another occasion were organised into two teams for a competition.

How important was feedback from the ICT systems to the learners?
Learners received instructional feedback when using 'Issues in English'. It appears that it was very important for them to get a high mark and for at least one learner observed, only a completely correct mark was felt to be satisfactory. Because the learner wanted to get a full mark, she repeated the exercise many times until she succeeded. The tutor said that he was reluctant to use software that provided feedback to learners, as he was concerned that learners' desire for full marks would not necessarily mean that they would learn more/better.

Did the learners' levels of ICT skills impact upon their learning?
There were two incidents where ICT skill levels interacted with the learning of literacy. Two learners with a high level of ICT skills spent much of one session in decorating their assignment sheet by inserting borders, drawing shapes, headings, changing colours, etc. rather than in completing the assignment. Another learner with a high level of literacy skills but poor ICT skills was stuck when using 'Issues in English' because she was not able to insert the cursor and add the punctuation mark where she wanted to put it.

ES1 – free-standing maths unit – Level 2

Background

There were 18 learners enrolled on this course, and the usual attendance was about four or five. The class lasted one and a half hours. There was poor attendance and punctuality in this class with different learners showing up for different sessions. The total number of observation units was 50, in 18 per cent of which ICT was not the predominant activity. There were very few ICT technical problems (1 per percent). All observed ICT use was of desktop computers. The main software used was office software (44 per cent), with some use of educational software (18 per cent) and of the Web for accessing information (10 per cent). Learners generally worked on their own and there was no observed use of small group work. The main purpose of ICT use was for learners to enter information (56 per cent), with some use concentrated on developing ICT skills (12 per cent) The tutor spent most time discussing work with individual learners (72 per cent) and a smaller proportion addressing the class as a whole (22 per cent).

1. Learning goals

What were the tutor's learning objectives?

The class is a free-standing mathematics unit in a practical skills course – this is a Level 2 course. The tutor said that these learners don't stay and so the class had become a form of drop in facility with individual support.

The use of spreadsheets and calculators was a compulsory part of this class, and the learners were expected to use them in their assignments. The use of spreadsheets and calculators was seen as an aspect of mathematics.

Session	ICT objectives	Numeracy objectives
1 and 2	Locate and select data from a supermarket website. Locate a file on the shared drive. Enter a formula into a spreadsheet and calculate unit cost. Fill down. Copy a spreadsheet and modify it.	Determine best buys by calculating the unit cost, using a spreadsheet. State how they know that their calculated unit costs are sensible/correct.
3	Enter a formula into a spreadsheet and calculate unit cost. To fill down. Be able to copy a spreadsheet and modify it.	Complete 'Best Buy' assignment – calculating the unit cost, using a spreadsheet. State how they know that their calculated unit costs are sensible/correct. Collect data for their second assignment.

How was the use of ICT integrated with the learning objectives?

There was a strong integration of ICT skills and numeracy in the objectives and the ICT skills taught were necessary for the achievement of the numeracy skills. Spreadsheets were seen as part of present day mathematics.

What were the forms of assessment used?

The tutor assessed both ICT and numeracy skills in a similar way: by talking with learners and making an informal assessment of their ability to do the tasks set.

2. Teaching

What happened in the sessions?

Session 1 (14/11/02)

Eight learners slowly came in and logged-on. The tutor gave individual instructions. He directed each learner to the intranet maths folder and the Excel template. He then told them to access the Tesco website, to note the prices of different types of goods into the Excel template and to work out the unit cost. The tutor circulated and helped learners individually. He explained the tasks again and ran through how to complete each step, in particular how to do the calculations. He spent most time with three learners who were motivated to complete the task. He made various attempts to get the other learners to take part, but they were unwilling and spent most time off task, chatting and surfing the Internet.

Session 2 (28/11/02)

Three learners came to this session, all arriving late. The tutor worked with the learners on a one-to-one basis. He talked them through the computer tasks, sometimes taking over control of the keyboard, discussed how to do the calculations and how to express the results in good English.

One learner started this project in this session, another learner had started it before and finished it in this session and the third learner had finished it during the previous session and printed it out for the tutor. The tutor introduced him to the next assignment, but he did not work on it. The other learners listened and participated in a short discussion about the next assignment.

Session 3 (12/12/02)

Four learners arrived rather late. The tutor gave them a course assignment related to cars. He gave them an observation sheet with four types of cars they had to observe, and he asked them to decide the sample size they were going to use; each elected for a sample size of 20. They then went outside the college in pairs to record the type of cars passing in order to provide data which they would enter into Excel and then produce a graph.

When the learners returned, the tutor directed learners separately to use Excel and told them, individually, what they had to do. The learners had met Excel before as it had been used in the previous assignment but the graphing feature was novel to most of them. The tutor went from learner to learner helping with problems. The focus of the work was getting to grips with Excel.

Learner A logged on with ease and went directly to Excel with confidence. The tutor told him to type in the labels of the types of cars and to enter the frequency of the observations of each type. He typed with speed and accuracy. The tutor demonstrated how to highlight cells and to create a chart. He understood what he had to do and worked swiftly, entering the title and the axis labels. He started to answer the questions on the assignment sheet but had a problem when asked which was the most popular type, as two types had the same frequency. He entered one type, but the tutor told him to put in both when he checked it later. He went on to calculate the fraction of the cars that were of the most popular type and express this as a percentage. He printed and saved his graph and also tidied up the Excel worksheet (centred numbers and altered column widths) and then printed and saved the spreadsheet. When interviewed he said that he had attended IT classes and really enjoyed computing. He said that it was good using the computers for graphs as it produced tidier results than drawing them by hand.

Learner B logged on and went to Excel. He needed help from the tutor, as he was not very proficient with Excel. The tutor took control of the mouse and showed him how to put in the headings, and then guided him in entering the frequencies. The tutor then asked him to highlight the table and find the chart option. The tutor then moved on to help another learner. The learner highlighted the frequencies but when he tried to create a chart, he did not get an appropriate graph. The tutor returned and again taking over the mouse helped him to create the graph and showed him how to label the axes and put in the headings. The tutor then went to another learner and when he returned, again took over the mouse in order to demonstrate how to tidy up the spreadsheet. B further tidied up the spreadsheet by making the columns all of equal width, then saved his work and printed the graph and spreadsheet off as these were needed for his portfolio. The learner said that it was very good when the tutor helped him, but that in some sessions the tutor did not have time to help him as he had to spend a lot of time with each person.

What was the tutor's style of teaching?
The tutor had a tutorial style of teaching: he used to give task instructions individually to learners. When a learner came in, he or she was asked to log-on and directed to the task. No presentation device was used for whole class presentations.

Learners were not reluctant to use computers but they were reluctant to experiment and the learners would wait for the tutor's help. A notable feature was the learners' dependence on the tutor for help – ICT seemed to enhance the teacher-centeredness of the class even though the tutor adopted a tutorial approach.

How were the necessary ICT skills taught?
ICT skills were taught on a one-to-one basis, examples observed included adding titles to columns, creating formulae, typing data, filling in forms, adjusting the width of columns, using the undo function. This might be done by explanation for those with better ICT skills, or by taking over control of the computer and demonstrating the procedure for those with poorer ICT skills.

How did the tutor manage the classroom?
The tutor used a tutorial style of teaching and whilst learners waited for tutor attention either no learning took place or learners would rely on each other to help. The style of teaching was affected by the small number of learners and by their poor attendance and punctuality.

3. ICT

How was ICT used in the classroom?
The use of Excel was in effect part of the requirements of the numeracy course. Instructions were always given orally or on paper, ICT was not used to present the instruction. There were no observations of the learners being directed to use the Excel help features.

Were there any situations where the use of ICT may have acted as a barrier to learning or teaching?
Because some learners were relatively unfamiliar with Excel and because of the tutorial style

of teaching, learners had to wait for the tutor to go to them and help them if they did not have the necessary ICT skills.

The use of ICT and a tutorial-style of teaching did not seem to work well together in this class. Possible factors were that these were very needy learners, the learners were relatively unfamiliar with Excel and the lack of encouragement in education generally to experiment. It may be that this was an inappropriate use of this style of teaching – perhaps more teacher-centred presentation of ICT skills would have been useful, but this was made difficult by a range of factors including the lack of a data projector, poor learner attendance and punctuality. The consequence of using a package that is unfamiliar to learners in what was almost a drop-in style workshop can potentially involve constant review of technical skills.

4. Learning
How did the learners work with each other?
The two tasks observed (determining best buys by calculating unit of cost and observing the frequency of types of cars) were not structured in such a way as to encourage ICT to be used in a collaborative fashion. The activities were set up for learners to work individually, but learners did ask each other for technical assistance.

Did the literacy level of learners impact upon their use of ICT?
The literacy level of the learners was quite low and they had problems with completing the numeracy tasks because they had to explain their actions and choices in writing. The tutor spent quite a lot of time helping them with what they needed to write. When one learner tried to use the spellcheck in Excel, the tutor suggested that it would not help him very much, and instead spelt out the word for him.

JN – numeracy – Level 1

Background
There were 22 learners enrolled on this course and the usual attendance was about 11. The class lasted three hours. The total number of observation units was 64, in 44 per cent of which ICT was not the predominant activity. There were very few ICT technical problems (1 per cent). The main style of use in this class was desktop computers with audio (33 per cent), with some use without audio (18 per cent) and some use of the desktop computer as a presentation device (5 per cent). Almost all use of ICT was of educational software. All use was by learners working individually on computers. The main purpose of ICT use was to input practice materials (33 per cent), some was reading practice material (12 per cent) and a little devoted to developing IT skills (6 per cent). The tutors main activity was addressing the class as a whole (73 per cent), with some time spent in discussion (8 per cent), or observation of learners (15 per cent).

1. Learning goals
What were the tutor's learning objectives?
This was a numeracy Level 1 course. The learning objectives included only numeracy objectives. There was no plan to teach ICT skills and computers were to be used as a way to practice numeracy skills taught in other sessions (usually the day before).

Session	Numeracy objectives
1	Work comfortably with long division. Know BODMAS (order of operations). Develop the concept of decimal place value – multiply by 10, 100 and 1000.
2	Use decimal place value – multiply decimals by 10, 100, 1000 – divide decimals by 10, 100, 1000. Multiply decimals by decimals – divide decimals by whole numbers.
3	Introduce fractions – different systems. Recognise equal fractions, top heavy and mixed fractions.
4	Revise fractional numbers and concept. Work on the topic 'of' – a fraction of a quantity to multiplying fractions.
5	Introduce percentage. Work with percentages of a quantity. Change percentage to fractions and decimals. Compare values across the three systems of percentage, decimal and fractions.

How did these match to the learners' goals?

There were a number of incidents that indicated that the learners liked working with ICT as a way of learning numeracy. One learner commented that it was the use of visual images that made computers enjoyable and another learner, who was observed to be withdrawn in whole-class teaching, worked with concentration when using the computer.

One learner said that the mathematics was too easy for her and that she was only taking this class because of her poor English skills. The software allowed her to work at her own pace, which was clearly faster than the rest of the class, but she said that she wanted something more challenging.

How was the use of ICT integrated with the learning objectives?

The numeracy objectives are primary in this class and ICT is used simply as a means for presenting and practicing mathematics, there are no ICT aims. The tutor said that since ICT was not the focus of the class then the ICT demands should be kept to a minimum so that attention was not drawn away from the main purpose of the class. The tutor stressed two particular advantages for using computers: the possibility of visual display (something she had found particularly useful in teaching fractions) and the possibility for learners to work through materials at their own pace and thus to provide the opportunity for exercise and reinforcement. The tutor had spent a lot of time identifying appropriate CD-ROMs (Numbers You Need and Numbers Disc) for this course and in carefully mapping elements of the materials to the topics to be taught. She felt that she needed this time to familiarise herself with the materials, to make sure that they could support her teaching objectives and to make sure that the learners would not need a high level of ICT skills to use the software.

To what extent was ICT seen as a basic skill?

The software demanded minimum ICT skills and so the tutor rarely taught ICT skills.

What were the forms of assessment used?

The software provided feedback, allowing learners to proceed at their own pace. The tutor provided feedback as she circulated around the class and she collected homework, marked it and returned it to learners.

2. Teaching

What happened in the sessions?

The numeracy teaching had been done previously in a non-computer classroom and then the computers were used for reinforcement. The room was small and there was insufficient room for learners to move off the computers and indeed the tutor said that she would have preferred a room in which learners could move from one situation to the other.

The main software being used was 'Numbers you need' from CTAD, originally developed for 10–15 year olds (Key Stages 3–4), but the tutor said that there had been no problems in using it with this group and they did not feel that it was 'childish'. The CD-ROM had no printable support materials or homework sheets , so the tutor used a different program to produce worksheets for homework. The tutor said that she felt confident in using this CD-ROM because it was stable and she knew it inside out, like a textbook.

The CD-ROM was easy to use, navigation was simple and learners felt confident because the system was very stable. There were a variety of levels allowing learners to work at their own pace, though the materials presented consolidation rather than challenge.

Session 1 (10/10/02)

There was no use of ICT in this session. Learners arrived slowly, took out books, pens and paper and started working. The tutor went around checking what each learner was doing and collecting their homework. The tutor briefly revised long division, writing examples on the board and talking learners through the steps and then asked them to do some examples on their own as she circulated and helped.

The tutor introduced the new topic ('order of operations'). She presented the topic, then got learners to work out some examples verbally in class and then to work on paper as the tutor circulated checking responses. The tutor gave then gave them a textbook exercise, which they learners worked on quietly. The tutor then collected their work and told them to go for a break.

After the break, the tutor introduced the topic of decimals and the number system, relating it to a discussion of money. She related decimals to division and finally discussed zero and positive and negative numbers. The tutor asked the learners to look at exercises in the textbook and the learners read out questions in turn and responded as a group. The tutor then wrote some questions on the board and circulated checking learners' answers.

The tutor dictated the record of work and learners confirmed and wrote it down.

Session 2 (16/10/02)

Learners slowly came in and logged on to the network. The tutor revised decimals and the number line on the board. She ran through a couple of worked examples and then the learners did exercises from the textbook during which time they worked individually. The tutor frequently interrupted and questioned learners, writing on the whiteboard and running through examples.

The tutor then asked all learners to log-on, to find the menu of CD-ROMs and to find 'Numbers You Need'. The tutor made sure that everybody had headphones and she asked the learners to start. The learners watched the slide show and the tutor then asked them to explain what it was about. She then related this to the work written on the board. The learners watched other slide shows and discussed them with the tutor, the tutor making connections with data on the whiteboard and the number line.

The tutor asked learners to switch to a new exercise on the CD-ROM about putting decimal numbers in order. She told the learners that as they cannot print anything out from the CD-ROM they should take notes. The learners worked on this exercise and the tutor walked round seeing each learner in turn. The tutor asked the learners to leave the computers and to open their textbooks. She discussed multiplication and division of decimals by 10 and 100, working through several examples with the class. The tutor then asked the learners to return to work on the computers on the multiplication and division sections of the CD-ROM.

Learners had a break for 20 minutes. When they came back they continued working individually on computers. The tutor walked around and checked their work and encouraged them to take notes, and to write down their answers. The tutor called the class together and introduced multiplication and division of decimals. The learners then did a paper and pencil exercise on this topic. The tutor asked the learners to go back to the computers and work on the section of the CD-ROM on the multiplication of decimals. The learners worked individually and many took notes on paper. The tutor interrupted them working at one point in order to show them how to use the index box in the software in order to find the section that they required.

The tutor asked learners to stop, get out their record of work and then she dictated what they were to write.

Session 3 (13/11/02)
Learners slowly came in, logged on and went onto the decimals section of the program.

The tutor called the class together and introduced the topic of fractions, through presentation on the whiteboard and through discussion with the class. The tutor asked learners to log-on and go to the fractions section of the program. The learners then went for a break and when they returned worked individually on the programs. The tutor circulated and encouraged the learners to take notes and to do calculations on paper before clicking on the answers.

The tutor called the class together, reviewed what they had done, and the learners completed their record of work and logged off.

Session 4 (20/11/02)
Learners slowly came in, and logged-on. They worked individually on computers and revised exercises that they had done in previous lessons. Some used headphones to listen to demonstrations.

The tutor brought the class together, revised the fractional number system briefly, and then introduced the main theme of the lesson – "of". She demonstrated several examples on the board, asking questions in order to encourage the learners to participate. The tutor then asked the learners to use their computers and to practice what they had just learnt. The tutor encouraged them to take notes and to write their answers on paper in order to keep a record of what they had done. The tutor circulated, observed and helped with individual problems.

Finally, the tutor asked the learners to complete their record of work and then set the homework.

Session 5 (04/12/02)

Learners slowly came in and logged-on. They worked individually on computers and revised exercises they had done in previous lessons. Some used headphones to listen to demonstrations. The tutor brought the class together, and revised fractions, percentages and decimals, and worked on changing between these notations. The learners had a break and when they came back worked on percentages from the 'Numbers You Need' package before the lesson was interrupted by a fire alarm.

What was the tutor's style of teaching?

The teaching was tutor-centred; the tutor had strong control of what happened in the class. She worked systematically through a series of tasks leading to content mastery: provided clear objectives at the beginning of each session, expected learners to learn specific things in a specific way, constantly revised and connected concepts together (such as decimals to fractions to percentages to number line), provided many examples of the same point until she was sure that every learner had understood, provided help and feedback and at the end of each session briefly summarised what had been learnt.

Concepts were taught for the first time in non-ICT sessions. The tutor started each ICT session by revising concepts learnt earlier and then she worked through several examples of what had been presented during the last non-ICT session, with the learners proposing possible answers and the class discussing these answers. She demanded active participation by everyone and if a learner was not participating then she would call on them by name. She always made sure that learners understood before moving on to another point. The tutor asked the learners to work on specific sections of the software and to take notes on paper. The learners then worked individually on the computers and there were few interactions among them, the class was very quiet.

How were the necessary ICT skills taught?

The only ICT skills needed in order to use the software chosen for the class were actions of ticking, dragging, typing words and moving forward and backward in the program. These actions were felt to be simple and the tutor did not set out to teach them. The tutor would teach specific ICT skills to individual learners if a problem arose, examples observed included: logging on, finding the program, navigating the program and increasing the sound level. On one occasion the tutor stopped the class in order to demonstrate how to use the index within the program in order to access specific materials.

How did the tutor manage the classroom?

The tutor addressed the whole class at the beginning of each session and worked through a series of problems on the whiteboard. Then when there was no-ICT use the tutor spent most of the time working in a whole class situation with the learners with the learners working on their own from worksheets or textbooks occasionally. Where ICT was used the tutor would ask learners to work individually on computers. There were few transitions to and from using computers, but when these did occur they were made smoothly, the tutor raised her voice to get attention, asked learners to turn their chairs and attend. The computer room was laid out so as to make it easy for learners to see the board and for the tutor to see what the learners were doing.

3. ICT

How was ICT used in the classroom?

ICT was used as another way of presenting and practicing numeracy concepts and provided learners the opportunity to work individually at their own pace.

Were there any situations where the use of ICT may have acted as a barrier to learning or teaching?

There were only minor problems with the use of ICT and there was no evidence of ICT acting as a barrier to learning or teaching. In one case where the program required a response in words rather than numerals some learners had difficulties because they misspelled the answer and on another occasion an answer was rejected because a learner put a full stop at the end of his answer.

4. Learning

How did the learners work with each other?

Learners worked on their own. The class was very quiet and there were only a few interactions among learners – principally about maths problems or navigating the software.

How important was feedback from the ICT systems to the learners?

The software used in these sessions provided immediate feedback to the learners and learners would repeat an exercise if they got it wrong. This often allowed learners to work at their own pace particularly when they were practicing topics that they understood, but where learners were dealing with topics that they did not understand then the feedback was not helpful.

Was ICT used in such a way as to enable a match to learners' learning styles or preferences?

There was some indication of meeting the needs of some learners for visual presentations, and for others to work at their own pace.

Did the literacy level of learners impact upon their use of ICT?

A few learners had problems where the software required a response in words rather than numbers, because of difficulties with spelling.

Appendix 2: **Pratt's teaching perspectives**[20]

Transmission

Effective teaching requires a substantial commitment to the content or subject matter. Good teaching means having mastery of the subject matter or content. Teachers' primary responsibilities are to represent the content accurately and efficiently. Learner's responsibilities are to learn that content in its authorised or legitimate forms. Good teachers take learners systematically through tasks leading to content mastery: providing clear objectives, adjusting the pace of lecturing, making efficient use of class time, clarifying misunderstandings, answering questions, providing timely feedback, correcting errors, providing reviews, summarising what has been presented, directing students to appropriate resources, setting high standards for achievement and developing objective means of assessing learning. Good teachers are enthusiastic about their content and convey that enthusiasm to their students. For many learners, good transmission teachers are memorable presenters of their content.

Apprenticeship

Effective teaching is a process of socializing students into new behavioral norms and professional ways of working. Good teachers are highly skilled practitioners of what they teach. Whether in classrooms or at work sites, they are recognised for their expertise. Teachers must reveal the inner workings of skilled performance and must translate it into accessible language and an ordered set of tasks which usually proceed from simple to complex, allowing for different points of entry depending upon the learner's capability. Good teachers know what their learners can do on their own and where they need guidance and direction; they engage learners within their 'zone of development'. As learners mature and become more competent, the teacher's role changes; they offer less direction and give more responsibility as students progress from dependent learners to independent workers.

Developmental

Effective teaching must be planned and conducted "from the learner's point of view". Good teachers must understand how their learners think and reason about the content. The primary goal is to help learners develop increasingly complex and sophisticated cognitive structures related to the content. The key to changing those cognitive structures lies in a combination of two skills: (1) teaching that engages learners with content while also challenging them to move from relatively simple to more complex forms of thinking, and (2) 'bracketing of professional knowledge' which allows learners time to construct their own understanding of the content. Questions, problems, cases, and examples form bridges that teachers use to transport learners from simpler ways of thinking and reasoning to new, more complex and sophisticated forms of reasoning. It is crucial, particularly in the initial stages of learning, that teachers adapt their professional knowledge to learners' levels of understanding and ways of thinking.

---

20. Taken from http://www.edst.educ.ubc.ca/faculty/pratt/DPtpsum.html – accessed 18 May 2004.

Nurturing

Effective teaching assumes that long-term, hard, persistent effort to achieve comes from the heart as much as it does from the head. People become motivated and productive learners when the standards for achievement are clear and accompanied by a balance of academic and emotional support. From a Nurturing point of view people are better at learning when they know that: (1) their learning efforts will be supported by both the teacher and their peers; (2) their achievement is acknowledged to be a product of their own effort and ability, rather than the benevolence of a teacher; and (3) their self-esteem and self-concept is not at risk during learning. From a Nurturing perspective, effective teachers do not lower their standards; nor do they excuse learners from doing what is required. Rather, effective teachers help learners set challenging but achievable goals, reinforce effort as well as achievement and acknowledge individual growth as well as absolute achievement.

Social Reform

Effective teaching seeks to change society in substantive ways. From the Social Reform point of view, the object of teaching is the collective rather than the individual. Good teachers awaken students to values and ideologies that are embedded in texts and common practices within their disciplines. Good teachers challenge the status quo and encourage students to consider how learners are positioned and constructed in particular discourses and practices. To do so, they analyse and deconstruct common practices for ways in which such practices perpetuate conditions that are unacceptable. Class discussion is focused less on how knowledge has been created, and more by whom and for what purposes. Texts are interrogated for what is said and what is not said; what is included and what is excluded; who is represented and who is omitted from the dominant discourse. Students are encouraged to take critical stances to give them power to take social action to improve their own lives and the lives of others. Critical deconstruction, though central to this view, is not an end in itself.

Appendix 3: **Research instruments**

Class tutor's pre-session report

Preliminary information

Tutor: **Organisation:**

Session: **Date:**

Please outline your lesson plan for this session, attach if already prepared, covering:
- Teaching objectives
- Learners' tasks and learning objectives
- Materials and tools (ICT: for example, class computer screen, particular software, www sites, own design software tasks, e-mail and ... Other media: for example, text books, worksheets, whiteboard, pen and paper and ...)

Please comment on the following:

- For this particular session, what are the main purposes of using ICT?

_____

- What are the planned patterns of teaching with ICT in this session?

_____

- For this session, what forms of presentation of teaching material will be used and how are these integrated with ICT presentation and use?

_____

- Please note any particular software to be used in this session.

_____

- Any additional comments about your use of ICT

_____

Thank you. Please email this report with your lesson plan to m.sanderson@ioe.ac.uk or post or fax them to M. Sanderson, NRDC Bedford Group, Room 709 Institute of Education, 20 Bedford Way, London WC1H 0AL. Fax no. 020 7612 6671

Classroom observation schedule

Research observers report

Code	Numbers		Software details and other material
Site		Classroom details	
Class tutorial	Enrolled	Usual	
Class & time		Today	

ICT use	Class context
ICSY Style of use	**CCTU** Tutor activities
ICTY Type of use	**CCSA** Learner activities
ICUS Users	**CCEQ** Non–ICT equipment
ICPU Purpose	
ICCP Computer problems	**Tutor observer:** **Research observer:**
ICCU ICT problems for user	name: name:

Research observers record

Time	ICSY	ICTY	ICUS	ICPU	ICCP	ICCU	CCTU	CCSA	CCEQ	Research observers record ACTION	Code: COMMENT	Learning goal
0930–0940												

Tutor-researcher observation report

Observer: **Observer's Institution:**

Tutor visited: **Institution visited:**

Session title: **Date:**

As you know, the purpose of the study is to build a picture of how different tutors in different classes use ICT in the teaching of basic skills and your report is an integral part of the study.

Please comment on the nature any particular teaching or learning events or moments involving ICT that occurred in the session with individual learners, groups or the whole class. It would be helpful if you could make a note of the time at which they occurred.

Some of the areas you may care to comment on in your observation report of the session include, for example: when and how did the tutor integrate computer activities into the teaching process and how did s/he make transitions to and from using computers with the class, groups or individual learners and with other materials. For what purpose did the tutor use computers in this lesson, for example, was it to motivate the learners or an activity, for teaching new basic skills material, as a means of practice, for the teaching of ICT skills?

Please email your completed report to m.sanderson@ioe.ac.uk

Thank you for your help.

Learner observation schedule

Code	Researcher	Classroom details	Software& other details
Site		Enrolled	
Class tutor (C)		Usual number	
Class & time		Today's number	

Rough notes on what has to be observed.
Time at the start of the observed event

Were the learners being observed – solitary, in pairs or in a group at the computer?
Was the work self-initiated by the learner/s or did the tutor instruct them to do it?
Did they ask the tutor before they started?

Was the whole class doing the same learning event?

Did the tutor assign the learners being observed to particular roles
e.g. one writing and the other accessing the computer?
Did they self elect to do the roles required?
Was there any discussion or dispute about this?

Did the tutor give them a hand out, text book etc. before the task started?
Did they have the necessary tools for the task?
Was there adequate room on the work surface to perform the task

Did they appear to understand what they were required to achieve?
Did they appear confident about tackling the work required?
Did they appear confident about the computer use involved?
Did they talk about what they had to achieve and how they would tackle it?
Did they disagree and then discuss and come to an agreement?

In achieving the goal of the event, the learners may have to do various tasks.
The following should be noted for each task done:

Classify the style of presentation (use the categories from the teacher observation)
Classify the type of use (use the categories from the teacher observation)

Note the onset time and define the nature of each task and incorporate the purpose of the computer use.

- Was the use of the computer to motivate the learners to do the task, motivate discussion ?
- Did the task involve new material to learn or apply new knowledge using only known ICT skills?
- Did it also require the use of new ICT skills?
- Was it an exercise to practice or apply previous knowledge (e.g. decimals) using previously acquired ICT skills?
- Did it also encompass new ICT skills?

Did the learners encounter any problems with the content material, the software, the hardware?

How did they resolve these – between themselves by trying various options, by asking someone else in the class, by asking the tutor?

Did the tutor notice they had problems and come over and help them?

Was the help given by telling them what to do or by discussing the problem and eliciting suggestions from them?

Did they achieve the task goal?

Did they receive feedback from the tutor, from the computer?

Did they discuss the feedback given and did it modify their strategy?

Next task: note the onset time and the information above

Note the time at the end of the learning event

Did they achieve the learning event's goal successfully or not?

Did they get feed back from the computer, from their peers, from the tutor?

What was their reaction?

Did they discuss what they has done?

What happened next?

Pro-forma for summaries of observational data

1. Learning goals

a   Describe the learning objectives of the sessions – this should be derived from the tutors pre-session report, lesson plans, interviews, meetings, and any feedback.

b   Provide any evidence of matches or mismatches between the tutor's learning objectives and the learners' needs/goals/objectives?

c   Describe how the teaching of ICT is integrated with the learning objectives. Describe how the teaching of ICT is integrated into the lesson plans. Describe the relationship of ICT and the content learning objectives, for example, which is seen as primary.

d   Describe any evidence of ICT being viewed as a basic skill, or as a subject in itself. Describe any evidence of progression in ICT skills being considered.

e   For ESOL or literacy classes provide any evidence of planning the use of ICT that takes into account the differing needs of these two audiences.

f   Describe the forms of assessment used for ICT and for literacy, numeracy and ESOL as appropriate. Provide any evidence that this impacts upon the design of the teaching sessions.

2. Teaching

a   Describe the teaching in the three sessions based on observation sheets, etc.

b   Provide any evidence about the tutor's perspective on teaching.
   (Refer to Pratt's classification:
   i. The Transmission Perspective: Effective Delivery of Content.
   ii. The Apprenticeship Perspective: Modelling Ways of Being.
   iii. The Developmental Perspective: Cultivating Ways of Thinking.
   iv. The Nurturing Perspective: Facilitating Self-efficacy.
   v. The Social Reform Perspective: Seeking a Better Society?)

c   Describe the tutor's style of teaching. Describe the way in which task instructions are given to the class. In particular provide any evidence of possible relationship between the use of ICT and the tutor's style teaching – does the tutor assimilate ICT to their normal teaching style, or does the use of ICT influence and change the tutor's teaching style?

d   Describe how are the necessary ICT skills are taught.

e   Describe how the tutor manages the classroom, and provide any evidence of ways in which this may be affected by the use of ICT.

f   Describe to what extent what happened in the classroom corresponded with the tutor's original plans. Provide any evidence that ICT impacted on this.

g   Provide any evidence that the relationship between ICT and content teaching in the learning objectives was achieved and to what extent this changed in practice.

3. ICT

a   Describe ways in which ICT was used in the classroom, based on observation sheets etc.

b   Provide evidence of any situations where ICT may have acted as a barrier to learning or teaching.

c   Describe any instances of technological failure and the consequences of this.

4. Learning

a   Describe how the learners worked with each other, in particular comment upon the extent to which learners worked alone or co-operated either on their own initiative or on the instruction of the tutor.

b   Describe any incidents that highlight the importance of feedback from the ICT to the learners.

This feedback might be instructional feedback (such as 'correct', 'wrong') or might be the responsiveness of the system (such as drawing a graph).

c   Provide any evidence of incidents in which the use of ICT may have matched learners' preferences for modes of learning (such as preference for visual over textual explanations).

d   Provide any evidence of the effect of the literacy level of learners impacting (either positively or negatively) upon their use of ICT.

e   Provide any evidence of the effect of learners' levels of ICT skills impacting (either positively or negatively) upon their learning of literacy, numeracy or ESOL.